THE SEE OF PETER AND THE VOICE OF ANTIQUITY

CRITICAL NOTES ON BISHOP COXE'S ANTE-NICENE FATHERS

BY

REV. THOMAS S. DOLAN

AUTHOR OF "PLAIN SERMONS"

WITH A PREFACE BY

HIS EMINENCE JAMES CARDINAL GIBBONS, D.D.

ST. LOUIS, MO., AND FREIBURG (BADEN)
PUBLISHED BY B. HERDER
1908

NIHIL OBSTAT.

F. G. HOLWECK,
Censor theologicus.

S. Ludovici, die 14. Martii 1908.

IMPRIMATUR.

✠ JOANNES J. GLENNON,
Archiepiscopus S. Ludovici.

S. Ludovici, die 14. Martii 1908.

239.34

D659

7105

—BECKTOLD—
PRINTING AND BOOK MFG. CO.
ST. LOUIS, MO.

PREFACE

This book is a refutation of Bishop Coxe's notes on the ante-Nicene Fathers, in so far as these notes call into question the ancient authority and prestige of the Apostolic See.

This refutation comprises principally, studies in the original texts of Clement of Rome, Ignatius, Irenæus, Hippolytus, Tertullian, Origen and Cyprian; with a view to correcting inaccurate readings, exposing bits of special pleading, textual distortions and historical misrepresentations.

The special exercise of jurisdiction outside of the diocese of Rome, on the part of Popes Clement I, Victor, Dionysius, Cornelius and Stephen in ante-Nicene times, is set forth and explained on the only one possible ground.

Dr. Coxe's "accounting" for the rise and development of the "papal system" is proven a miserable fabrication, having no relation to history.

His contention that the Papacy rests upon the "Forged Decretals," is disposed of.

His declaration that the East never ac-

iii

cepted the "Petrine claims," is refuted by ample and unquestionable oriental testimony.

Father Dolan being a man of natural ability, perfected by long training, and broadened by large erudition, I doubt not that this scholarly work of his will be gladly received and widely read.

I commend this work to the many who have the edition of Dr. Coxe's ante-Nicene Fathers, as well as to all interested in things Catholic and historical.

J. Card. Gibbons.

INTRODUCTION

The writer is fully aware that the subject matter of the present volume has been treated ably by theologians and controversialists. Yet, for reasons which shall be set forth presently, he thinks the following pages opportune, and hopes that they may prove helpful in the discussion of a doctrine, which so sharply distinguishes Catholicism from Protestantism.

Some years ago, a translation of the ante-Nicene Fathers was published by Charles Scribner's Sons of New York City. This publication was a reprint of the well known Oxford and Edinburgh translations. The series produced in New York was, unfortunately, edited by Bishop Coxe, the then Protestant-Episcopal Bishop of western New York. That Dr. Coxe was a man of considerable and varied learning, must be admitted readily; but just as readily must it be maintained, that he had very little critical faculty—or if he had that faculty in any generous measure, it is most effectively concealed in his notes on the ante-Nicene Fathers. His animus toward the Catholic Church, was such as to vitiate any work which he might have essayed upon those points, which differentiate the sect to which he belonged, from the Universal Church. Any patristic reference to the See of Rome, and its position of pre-eminence in the episcopate, produces in Dr. Coxe a sort of frenzy; and by every sort of expedient, he endeavors to weaken, minimize or destroy in the reader's mind, the obvious meaning of the text. On occasion, he dismisses a text distinctly favorable to the Catholic doctrine concerning the Pope, with the remark, that "the passage is undoubtedly spurious," without however, offering anything that possibly could be taken as a proof of his assertion. His method at times betrays him into pitiable situations. This is painfully evident in his efforts to coerce Irenæus and Cyprian into his way of estimating the power of the Roman Pontiffs, in the first ages of the Church.

Now there has been another edition of this same series of Ante-nicene Fathers published within the last two or three years, with all Dr. Coxe's notes intact. This edition has been widely advertised, and it is common

knowledge, that Catholic priests in considerable numbers have patronized it. It has
been followed by editions of the Nicene and
post-Nicene Fathers. It is only fair to state,
that the editors of the two latter series,
though not sympathetic with any distinctively
Catholic positions, are men of greater
breadth and more critical scholarship than
the estimable Dr. Coxe.

It appears to the writer, that the work of
examining and refuting Bishop Coxe's notes,
by appeals to the undisputed texts of the
ante-Nicene Fathers, would be acceptable,
and perhaps of assistance to the younger
clergy, among whom there is an unmistakable
intellectual stir. I might add, that there are
serious reasons, why such a work should find
its way into the hands of the educated laity.

The edition of the Fathers now under consideration, open though it be to justly unfav-
orable criticism, is nevertheless a boon. Although the number of Catholic priests who
could deal familiarly with the Latin Fathers
in their own idiom, is by no means inconsiderable, yet, for a great many, the perusal of
the original texts, would take on a laborious
character. This observation applies to the
Greek Fathers with much greater force.
Hence it is of no mean advantage to have

facile access to so much Patristic literature,
as the English edition affords. It is expedient however, if not really necessary, to
have at hand some antidote for the errors,
the prejudice, the manifestly false, if not
dishonest interpretations, the distortion of
texts and the bits of foolish special pleading,
that here and there disfigure the work. That
antidote, this unpretentious volume, endeavors in some little measure to supply.

T. S. D.

St. Mary's,
   Laurel, Md.,
      Feb., 1908.

CONTENTS

CHAPTER I

PETER, BISHOP OF ROME — CLEMENT, TO THE CORINTHIANS

CHAPTER II

IGNATIUS — IRENÆUS

CHAPTER III

TERTULLIAN AND ORIGEN

ix

CHAPTER IV

HIPPOLYTUS

CHAPTER V

CYPRIAN

THE SEE OF PETER AND THE VOICE OF ANTIQUITY

CHAPTER I

ST. PETER, BISHOP OF ROME. CLEMENT TO THE CORINTHIANS

I

"When the Church was thrown upon her own resources, first local disturbances gave exercise to Bishops, and next ecumenical disturbances gave exercise to Popes; and whether communion with the Pope was necessary for Catholicity, would not and could not be debated, till a suspension of that communion had actually occurred. It is not a greater difficulty, that St. Ignatius does not write to the Asian Greeks about Popes, than that St. Paul does not write to the Corinthians about Bishops. And it is a less difficulty, that the Papal supremacy was not formally acknowledged in the second century, than that there was no formal acknowledgment on the part of the Church of the doctrine of the Holy Trinity, till the fourth. No doctrine is defined till it is violated."

1

"And in like manner, it was natural for Christians to direct their course in matters of doctrine, by the guidance of mere floating, and as it were, endemic tradition, while it was fresh and strong; but in proportion as it languished or was broken up in particular places, did it become necessary to fall back upon its special homes, first the Apostolic Sees, and then the See of Peter." [1]

These words from the pen of Cardinal Newman, shed floods of light upon a dogma which has been impugned, traduced and reviled most thoroughly, by our separated brethren. The line of argument adopted by our Anglican opponents, namely, that the Papal idea was not sufficiently in evidence during the first ages of the Church, to warrant its acceptance on their part, cannot well endure critical inspection. The same process of argumentation, logically forces the adherents of the Anglican position, to call into question the consubtantiality of Jesus Christ with the Father; for this point of doctrine was not only storm-swept from the first age of Christianity, but (as Newman observes above), it was not defined until the fourth century. And even after the august assembly of Nice had promulgated its symbol, the

[1] Newman's "Development," Cap. IV, Sect. III.

homoüsios was not only repudiated by a considerable number of bishops, as for instance the Eusebians convened at Antioch, about the middle of the fourth century, but at the same period bishops, intentionally the most orthodox, juggled (if I may be allowed the word) with the symbol, after most curious fashions, as is evident from their letters to one another. No one acquainted with Patristic literature, will deny, that the language of a number of the Ante-nicene Fathers concerning the homoüsios was such, as they would not have used after the symbol had been imposed.

The real reason of the Anglican attitude toward the Holy See is simply this. The doctrine of Papal Supremacy was the point of contact, when the lusts of an English king —a carrion beast, as Father Robert Hugh Benson so fitly calls him—collided with the Universal Church.   As a result of the impact, the Cathedra Petri unimpaired continued to exercise its Christ-conferred prerogatives, and the English Church severely wounded from the shock, declined from her former self, and became what she is to-day, a church of shreds and patches.   Her apologists and theologians in their efforts to make her position tenable, must of necessity endeavor to demonstrate the spuriousness of Papal

claims. With a foolish temerity they appeal
to the primitive age of Christianity. That appeal is fatal to their pretensions. "To be
deep in history," says Newman, "is to cease
to be a Protestant."

The Right Reverend Bishop Coxe begins
his labors in the field of Patrology, by con-
ceding that the martyrdom of Sts. Peter
and Paul at Rome *"seems historical,"* and
by declaring that Clement of Rome "was the
natural representative of St. Paul and even
of his companion St. Peter."

Though some few Protestant writers have
attacked the tradition, which points to the
residence of St. Peter in Rome as bishop of
that city, and his glorious martyrdom there,
their efforts to break down the superabun-
dant testimony afforded by Fathers, historians and a universal belief in the Church,
have failed most dismally. It is a matter
of marvel, that in the face of such testimonies as those of Irenæus,[1] Tertullian,[2]
Cyprian,[3] Eusebius,[4] and a host of post-
Nicene authorities, such as Theodoret, Je-
rome, Augustine, Ambrose, Leo the Great,
Gregory the Great and others, that a handful

[1] Contra Haeres. lib. IV, C. 3.
[2] Contra Marcion, lib. III.
[3] Ep. LIV ad Cornel.
[4] Lib. II, C. 23. Lib. III, C. 4.

of moderns would brave the task of keeping
the Prince of the Apostles and the Rock upon
which the fabric of the Church is reared, out
of Rome.   To state, in the face of the overwhelming testimony, proving the residence
of St. Peter at Rome, as its bishop, and his
martyrdom there that they only ''seem'' historical, is at once an evidence of pronounced
bias, and an absence of critical scholarship,
for that scholarship takes the correct measure of historical documents.

II

Bishop Coxe takes care to observe in a
footnote anent the inscription of the famous
Clementine epistle to the Corinthians, that
the latter requested Clement to write the
epistle.   The inference to be drawn is, that
Clement would not have interfered otherwise in the affairs of another church.   This
little note of the ingenious Dr. Coxe is un-
fortunate for his case.   It is unquestionably
true, that Pope Clement was asked for the
weight of his authority, and the light of his
wisdom to cure the sedition which then rent
the church of Corinth.   ''We feel,'' writes
Clement, ''that to some extent, we have not
been prompt enough, in giving our attention
to the affairs concerning which you have

consulted us."[1] Instead, however, of regarding this as a fact, which made the letter permissible, it must be looked upon simply as an appeal to the See of Peter. And in order to settle one's mind in the conviction, that this and nothing else was intended, it will be sufficient to read the text of the letter itself, keeping in view the fact, that John the Apostle and Evangelist was still alive at Ephesus. Were there no special prerogatives attaching to the See of Rome, what would have been more to be expected, than an appeal of the faithful presbyters and people at Corinth to the apostle whom Jesus loved. There is no reasonable explanation of the Corinthians overlooking the sole survivor of the Twelve, save that Rome was pre-eminent in authority. Bishop Coxe's explanation of the action of the Corinthians going to Rome instead of to Ephesus, is a geographical one; for, as he says, "Rome was of easier access." Notwithstanding the famous road system of the empire, which made Rome of such facile access, the statement of Dr. Coxe is false; and as a reason it is childish. The voyage across the Ægæn Sea from Corinth to Ephesus, was far shorter than the voyage over portions of

[1] Ep. Clem. ad Romanos. C. I.

the Mediterranean and up the Adriatic, or around by the west coast of Italy. If it were a question of travel by land, even the roundabout route from Corinth, up through Greece, Macedonia, across Thrace and down through Asia-Minor, to the seat of the venerable apostle, would have been much shorter than any conceivable journey to Rome.

Dr. Coxe maintains that there is textual evidence that the epistle was the result of many at Rome deliberating, and writing as it were in common. Subsequently he flatly contradicts himself, by admitting the Clementine authorship. The intelligent perusal of this document reveals *one man* writing, a man *conscious of authority, a man meaning to teach, to censure sedition in the Church, to reprove and condemn the guilty, and to recall them to the path of righteousness.* There is no arrogant display of prerogative —Clement was a saint—but the humility discernible in the letter closely resembles that of Paul, a humility namely, which in no way minimized apostolic authority. He upbraids the Corinthians for their "envy, strife and sedition, persecution and disorder, war and captivity. The worthless have risen against those worthy of respect and honor, those of no reputation against the renowned, the foolish against the wise, the young against the old. Righteousness and peace have departed from you. Everyone abandons the fear of God. . . . Ye therefore who are guilty, arousing this sedition, submit yourselves to the presbyters, receive the correction so as to repent, bending the knees of your hearts. Learn to be subject, putting away the proud and arrogant self-confidence of your tongues. . . . Send back speedily to us in peace and with joy these our messengers . . . that they may the sooner announce to us the peace and harmony we so earnestly desire and long for among you,'' etc. Are these the expressions of a bishop unconscious of any special authority, when addressing the faithful outside the territorial limits of his diocese. I think not. The best evidences for our contention [1] are the words of the ancient Pope himself, without reinforcement of any pleading. We may fittingly call the letter of Clement the first historic exercise of the Papal prerogative in the Church. It is not surprising to one familiar with the document, to read these words from the pen of Salmon, who can hardly be suspected of Papal leanings:

[1] Ep. ad Rom.   Cap. LVIII, LIX.

"He (Clement) as bishop of that church which was founded by the apostles speaks authoritatively, and thus shows the first beginnings of pontifical authority."[1] The same admission is made by one, who, though a Protestant, cannot close his eyes to the Papal character of the letter.[2] A fact of unquestionable importance in this connection is the profound reverence and esteem with which this letter was popularly regarded. Eusebius tells us that "this epistle great and admirable, which he (Clement) wrote in the name of the church at Rome to the church at Corinth, . . . has been publicly read in many churches, both in old times and also in our own day."[3] "Through this letter," says the erudite Dr. Shahan, "more than through any other early document, the note and criterion of 'apostolicity' was forced upon the churches. The Church of Rome has earned many titles to the gratitude of mankind, but none older or more venerable than this first authoritative interpretation of the constitution of the Catholic Church."[4]

[1] Introduc. to Study of N. T., p. 646.
[2] Shaff Creeds of Christendom.   Vol. II, p. 158.
[3] Hist. Eccl. III. 16.
[4] Beginnings of Christianity, p. 101. Dr. Shahan adds that Clement's decision was unasked for. This is not accurate. Corinth appealed to Rome.

CHAPTER II

I

"The epistle of St. Ignatius to the Romans," says Dr. Coxe, "is utterly inconsistent with any conception on his part, that Rome was the residence and see of a bishop, holding any other than friendly relations with himself. . . . Think of what use would have been made of it, had the words he addresses to the Smyrneans (cap. viii),[1] to strengthen their fidelity to Polycarp, been found in his letter to the Romans, especially, as in this letter we first find the use of the phrase 'Catholic Church' in patristic writings."

It is difficult to grasp how the foregoing note could be written by a man acquainted with the Ignatian letters. A careful inspection of the various inscriptions of the epistles to the Ephesians, the Magnesians, the Trallians, the Philippians, the Philadelphians and the Smyrneans, reveals the fact, that they are almost identical one with an-

[1] Ep. ad Smyrn.

10

other. The inscription of his letter to the Romans is altogether unique. Before studying it in some detail, it would be well for the reader to remember, that Ignatius neither in this nor in any other of his letters, is writing upon the position of the Roman bishop. The reference which he makes to Rome's position in the Church is incidental. The following is a literal translation of part of the said inscription: "Ignatius, who is also called Theophorus, to the Church, which is sanctified and enlightened by the will of God, who formed all things that are according to the faith and love of Jesus Christ our God and Savior; the Church which is pre-eminent in the seat of the region of the Romans, and which is worthy of God, worthy of honor, worthy of the highest beatitude, worthy of praise, worthy of credit, worthy of being esteemed as most holy, and which presides over the congregation of charity." Dr. Coxe adopts what the writer regards as a weak rendition of the phrase translated above as, "which is pre-eminent in the seat of the region of the Romans." Cardinal Newman renders the same very acceptably as follows: "Which holds the dignity of the first seat." The original reads as follows: " ἥτις καὶ προκάθηται ἐν τότω χωριον ρωμαίων." It should be observed that the verb προκάθημαί, according to all lexicographers, signifies I rule, I am pre-eminent, I protect, I defend, I sit in the first place, I preside. The rendition found above, "which presides over the congregation of charity," is from the Latin text, "quae coetui caritatis praesidet," as being less obscure than the Greek, which literally turned into English, would mean "which presides over love." Since then, Ignatius refers to dignity of place, presidency, pre-eminence, solely in his letter to the Romans, it is a most legitimate inference, that the explanation of his reference is the fact, that he regarded Rome as the center of ecclesiastical honor and jurisdiction. By the "coetui caritatis" must be understood the Universal Church, for surely such a term could not have been meant to point out the special and distinguishing character of the diocese of Rome, when all the churches to which Ignatius addresses himself, were at peace and in possession of the "sacramentum unitatis." In the course of this short epistle, Ignatius is careful to observe, that he would not presume to lay commands upon the faithful at Rome, since they were the spiritual progeny of the blessed Apostles Peter and Paul. It would be idle to lay too much stress upon this bit of evidence drawn from the Ignatian letter, but such as it is, it abundantly proves the falsehood contained in the note of Dr. Coxe.

II

Students of early Church history will readily recall the fact, that during the Aurelian persecution, Pothinus, who occupied the bishopric of Lyons, sent Irenæus, then a presbyter of the same diocese, to Rome, with letters to Pope Eleutherus, concerning the Montanist heretics. Dr. Coxe says "that he (Irenæus) had the mortification of finding the Montanist heresy patronized by the Bishop of Rome." He adds the following gem: "Let it be noted here, that, so far from being 'mother and mistress' of even the Western Churches, Rome herself is a mission of the Greeks; . . . Lyons checks the heretical tendencies of the Bishop at Rome; . . . and Latin Christianity, when it begins to appear, is African, not Roman. It is strange that those who have recorded this great historical fact, have so little perceived its bearings upon Roman pretensions in the Middle Ages and modern times." [1] We must refresh the reader with

[1] Ante-Nic. Fathers. Vol. I, p. 309.

just a bit more of Dr. Coxe's history (?).
"It is a striking example of divine economy,
that the see of Rome was allowed to exhibit
its fallibility at this time, very conspicuously,
and not only to receive the rebukes of
Irenæus, but to accept them as wholesome
and necessary; so that the heresy of Eleutherus and the spirit of Diotrephes in Victor, have enabled reformers ever since, even
in the darkest days of pontifical despotism,
to testify against the manifold errors patronized by Rome. Hilary and other Gal-
licans have been strengthened by the example of Irenæus, and by his faithful words of
reproof and exhortation, to resist Rome,
even down to our own times." [1]

The statement of Dr. Coxe that the letters
to Eleutherus which Irenæus carried to Rome,
were "letters of remonstrance" [2] is purely
gratuitous. It has not the merest semblance
of historical foundation. The same is absolutely true of his statement concerning the
heretical leanings of Pope Eleutherus. It
requires an abundance of blinding charity,
which the writer never hopes to possess, to
believe Dr. Coxe honest, after reading the
above quoted notes. The introduction of

[1] Ante-Nic. Fathers, Ibid. 310.
[2] Ibid. 309.

the famous letter of Pothinus is preserved
to us by Eusebius, and as the candid reader
will observe, it has all the requisite charac-
teristics of a letter of protest to a man—a
bishop—suspected of nursing heresy in the
bosom of the Church. "We pray, Father
Eleutherus, that you may rejoice in God in
all things and always. We have requested
our brother and comrade to carry this letter
to you, and we beg you to hold him in esteem, as zealous for the covenant of Christ.
For if we thought that office could confer
righteousness on anyone, we should commend him to you among the first, as a presbyter of the Church which is his position." [1]
Apart from this introduction, the letter is
entirely lost, and there is a serious quarrel
among historical critics, concerning the trend
of the same document. The more common
view among scholars is, that far from remon-
strating with Eleutherus because of his fa-
voring the Montanists, the Gallic martyrs
and their bishop begged Eleutherus to be
kind in his judgment of the Montanists, and
by allowing them the fellowship of other
Christians, to keep peace within the bosom
of the Church. There is very little in the
way of evidence to support this view. The

[1] Euseb. Hist. Eccl. V. 5.

statement of Eusebius, that the Gallic martyrs sent an *orthodox* [1] epistle to Eleutherus,
is perhaps sufficient proof that the letter
from Lyons was an *appeal* to Rome against
any toleration of the Montanist heresy.
The Montanists appealed to the See of Peter,
and we may assume without doing violence
to history, that the letter of the Gallic martyrs was a counter appeal. This letter is
called by Eusebius πρέσβεία, which can never
mean a simple communication, much less a
letter of reproach, since the idea of reverence or honor is always included in the word.
Incidentally we may remark, that this very
πρέσβεία, indicates thus early a "looking
up to Rome." [2]   Had Eleutherus been suspected of leniency toward Montanism, surely
Eusebius would have given at least a pass-
ing notice to the fact. No historian suggests
any infidelity on the part of that Pope. We
plead guilty to not wishing to regard Dr.
Coxe in the capacity of historian. I have
been unable to discover upon what ground
Dr. Coxe declares the Roman Church to have
been a mission of the Greeks in the time of
Irenæus. The reconciliation of such a posi-

[1] Euseb. Hist. Eccl. V. 3.
[2] Dr. McGiffert's notes on Euseb., V. 4, are of value in
this connection.

tion of the Roman Church, with the excommunication of the Eastern Churches by Pope Victor, is a task that no one acquainted with the history of the period would dare attempt. The action of Victor was unquestionably wrong; and proceeded as much perhaps from an impetuous temper, as from religious zeal. The time of celebrating Easter was far too trivial a circumstance, about which to endanger the peace of the Church. The action of Irenæus after he had succeeded Pothinus in the see of Lyons, in admonishing the Pope of the consequences of his action, was just and proper. There was no question of anything save a disciplinary enactment. The *power* of Victor was not called into question, and history tells us that he not merely threatened the Eastern Churches with excommunication, for differing with the West in the matter of celebrating the paschal fast and communion, but that he actually excommunicated them. This is unmistakable from the text of Eusebius: "ἀκοινωνήτους πάντας ἄρδην τοὺς ἐκεῖσε ανακηρυττών ἀδελφούς." [1] I cannot see how these words can be construed into a mere threat. Their literal and obvious meaning is, that he declared all the brethren there (in the dioceses of Asia)

1 Euseb. Hist. Eccl. V. 24.

wholly (ἄρδην) excommunicate. The historian
Socrates confirms this view. "Victor
Bishop of Rome, under the influence of a
very ardent zeal, promulgated a sentence
of excommunication against the Quartodeci-
mans in Asia."[1] The bishops who found
fault with the rash policy of Victor, in no
wise questioned his power, for as says Eusebius: "They begged him to remember the
things of peace and of fraternal unity and
of charity."[2] There was an unquestionable
consciousness on the part of Victor, that he
had an eminent right to demand obedience
of the Eastern Churches. His act of excommunication makes this clear, and the fact
that his authority, though criticised, was not
disputed even by the severest of his critics,
is I think, an undeniable proof of the general recognition of Rome's place in the
Church. To admonish a superior is not inconsistent with full recognition of his power.
The advices and reproofs administered to
Popes by a St. Bernard, and a St. Catherine
of Sienna, at times when the Papacy was supreme in both the spiritual and temporal
orders, were not regarded as questionings
of the papal prerogative.

[1] Socrat. Hist. Eccl. V. 22.
[2] Euseb. Hist. Eccl. V. 24.

Dr. Coxe devotes much labor to an attempt at explaining away the well-known passage, found in the third book of the treatise of Irenæus against the various heresies of his day. "Since it would be very wearisome in a book such as this," runs the passage, "to enumerate the successions of all the churches, . . . we point out the tradition handed down from the Apostles of the *greatest*, the *most ancient* and *universally known* church established at Rome by the two most glorious Apostles Peter and Paul. For because of its pre-eminent authority, it is necessary, that every church, that is, the faithful everywhere, should resort to this church, in which by universal consent, the apostolic tradition has been preserved unimpaired." It is idle to speculate on what the Greek text may have been, since that text is hopelessly lost. The Latin is clumsy, and distinctly lacking in classical flavor. "Ad hanc enim ecclesiam propter potiorem principalitatem, necesse est omnem ecclesiam convenire, hoc est, eos qui sunt undique fideles, in qua semper ab his, qui sunt undique, conservata est ea, quae est ab Apostolis traditio." [1] I have ventured to render "ab his qui sunt undique," "by universal consent." I have not found

[1] Iren. Advers. Haeres. lib. III, Cap. 4.

this translation anywhere given, yet I can
see no injustice to the text in making this
rendition. The sentence would be undoubtedly clearer, by the omission of the phrase
in question, yet it is found in every codex.
Independently of the textual difficulty suggested by these few words, the quotation
taken as a whole can mean only one thing.
It is a simple declaration of Rome's pre-
eminence—the greatest and most ancient
church—a declaration that Rome is the
special repository of apostolic tradition; and
a declaration finally that all the churches
must be in communion with the see of Rome,
in order to share in the "sacramentum
unitatis."

Let us attend now to some of the ingenious efforts of Dr. Coxe. The translation
of the passage now under consideration, as
it stands in the text edited by Dr. Coxe, is
very obscure. He repudiates it, and furnishes another with an interesting but utterly groundless paraphrase. "For it is
necessary for every Church (that is to say,
the faithful from all parts) to meet in this
Church, on account of the superior magis-
tracy (of the Empire); in which Church, by
those who are from all places, the tradition

of the apostles has been preserved." [1] Thus Dr. Coxe turns the passage of Irenæus, and I fancy that he breathed more easily as he finished the struggle. "The authors of the Latin translation," he says, "may have designed the ambiguity, which gives the ultramontane party an apparent advantage; but it is an advantage which disappears as soon as it is examined, and hence I am content to take it as it stands. . . . The Latin text answers every purpose of the author's argument, and is fatal to the claims of the Papacy. Let me recur to the translation given *in loco,* from a Roman Catholic, and this will be seen at once. For he thus renders it, 'In this Church, ever, by those who are on every side, has been preserved that tradition which is from the apostles. For to this Church on account of the more potent principality it is necessary that every Church resort.' The greatness of Rome, that is, as capital of the Empire, imports to the local Church a superior dignity. . . . Everybody visits Rome; hence you find there faithful witnesses from every side; and their united testimony it is, which preserves in Rome the pure apostolic tradition." [2]

[1] Ante-Nicene Fathers. Vol. I, p. 461.
[2] Ante-Nicene Fathers. Vol. I, pp. 460 & 461.

Dr. Coxe's remark about the designing proclivities of the authors of the Latin translation, is too purely gratuitous to deserve any notice here. The translation to which he refers as that of a Roman Catholic, is the rendition of Dupin—notoriously sympathetic with Gallicanism and largely antipapal—hence not representatively Roman Catholic. Dupin was a scholar of magnificent attainments, but with very definite prejudices in an anti-Roman direction. Notwithstanding all that may be said against him as a Catholic witness, however, and notwithstanding Dr. Coxe's devotion to the same great scholar, Dupin's translation of the much discussed passage of Irenæus gives absolutely no support to Dr. Coxe's position.

"The greatness of Rome, that is as capital of the Empire," according to our sagacious editor, gave the local church an ecclesiastical prominence. The center of pagan power and pagan iniquity lent nothing of prestige to the local ecclesiastical authority. Ecclesiastical dignity and power do not necessarily follow civil prominence. The see of Canterbury was always superior to that of London. We have no historical ground for supposing that there was such an influx of visiting Christians to Rome at the time of Irenæus, as Dr. Coxe states, and (be it said with reverence) there were reasons of a very grave character, why Christians who were not forced to go there, should carefully remain away. The Rome of the period was not the pleasantest rendezvous for the faithful. The faith was kept at Rome, according to Dr. Coxe by those who came there from all quarters. She was the mirror of the Catholic world, according to his pleasant way of putting things, but she was not the Sun dispensing her own light to other churches. From the Doctor's attitude, (had it any foundation) we would be forced to conclude, first, that Rome unlike Alexandria, Jerusalem, Antioch and the other primitive sees, required for the maintenance of orthodoxy a continuous influx of faithful from abroad. Secondly, her foundation by the blessed Apostles Peter and Paul, who watered with their blood the seed they had planted there, had no special influence in keeping pure the burden of their teaching. Thirdly, that the terms "greatest, most ancient and universally known Church," applied to Rome by Irenæus, really count for little or nothing. Lastly, I might add that even the visitors in their turn failed to keep Rome in proper condition, for nobody will hazard the assertion that they grew less as time went on, and in spite of their increase, Rome went to the bad anyhow. All this, I think, makes evident to the fair-minded reader, that the ideas of Dr. Coxe upon the famous testimony of St. Irenæus, had no reality save as they floated about in the muddled waters of his imagination.

"Rome," says Dr. Coxe, "takes all into her power, and may dictate to all churches what they are to believe, however novel or contrary to the torrent of antiquity in the teachings of their own founders and great doctors in all past time." [1] Hard words these indeed, yet not surprisingly so from the child of that apostate daughter of Rome. What marvel that the child should imitate the mother. And yet the pity of it! For that mother was the Church of an Augustine, a Lanfranc, a Dunstan, an Anselm and an á Becket. O, the pity of it, that in her apostasy such darkness o'erspread the land. "Jerusalem hath grievously sinned, and therefore she has become unstable; all that honored her have despised her because they have seen her shame. Her filthiness is upon her feet and she hath not remembered her

[1] Ante-Nicene Fathers. Vol. I, p. 461.

end." [1]   Yes, Rome takes all into her power,
and by her embrace gives that support, which
is hers by Divine commission to communi-
cate: "Tu aliquando conversus, confirma
fratres tuos." She takes all into her power,
but not to dictate what is novel or contrary to
antiquity, but rather to preserve intact the
deposit of Revelation by her definitions, to
separate the wheat from the cockle, and to
protect her little ones from being "tossed
to and fro, carried about by every wind of
doctrine." The famous text of Irenæus to
which we have just devoted ourselves, re-
ceives a striking interpretation and emphasis from these words of Augustine of Hippo.
"From the dunghill was Peter lifted up as
was Paul; when they suffered death they
were held in contempt: now, the earth having
been enriched by them, and the cross of the
Church springing up, behold, all that is noble
and princely in the whole world, even the
emperor himself, cometh to Rome, and
whither does he hasten? to the temple of
the emperor, or the memorial of the fisherman?" [2]

[1] Lament of Jeremias. Cap. I.
[2] Aug. in Ps. CXLI.

CHAPTER III

I

Bishop Coxe introduces us to the study of
Tertullian by some amazing declarations.
In his introductory note he assures us that
"at the close of the second century the
Church in Rome was an inconsiderable
though prominent member of the great fed-
eration of Christian Churches, which has its
chief seats in Alexandria and Antioch." [1]
This came to me as a surprise. Irenæus, a
contemporary of the period of Rome's incon-
siderableness, tells me that among the
churches, Rome is "maxima, antiquissima et
ab omnibus cognita." Bishop Coxe of the
nineteenth century tells me that the Roman
Church of the time had little or no distinction. As the Bishop has not earned a reputation for fair historical discussion, I am content to abide by the word of St. Irenæus.

Refreshed and stimulated by this flight,
the learned Dr. Coxe, after enumerating

[1] Ante-Nicene Fathers. Vol. III, p. 4.

26

Tertullian, Cyprian and Augustine as the great founders of the Carthaginian school of theology, informs us that, "Providentially" not one of these illustrious doctors died in communion with the Roman See, pure though it was and venerable at that time." [1] It is a matter of history that Tertullian died a heretic, in communion therefore with no orthodox see. There is no possible way of ascertaining whether St. Cyprian died in communion with Rome or not. St. Augustine thinks it probable that he did. It is a characteristic piece of assurance on the part of Dr. Coxe, to state without qualification that he did not. The same learned Doctor's declaration that Augustine died out of the Roman communion is unqualifiedly false. The fact that Cyprian has been numbered among the saints, and has been honored upon our altars for so many centuries, argues a strong probability that he was reunited to the Holy See before his martyrdom. The following extract from St. Augustine's letter to Vincentius [2] is of both interest and value in this connection. "The statement that Cyprian entertained opinions at variance with those approved by the constitution and practice

---

[1] Ante-Nicene Fathers.   Vol. III, p. 4.
[2] Ep. XCIII.

of the Church, is found, not in canonical
Scripture, but in his own writings, and in
those of a Council; and though in those same
writings it is not found, that he corrected
those views, it is by no means an unreason-
able supposition that he did correct them, and
this fact perhaps may have been suppressed
by those who were too much pleased with
the error into which he fell, and were un-
willing to lose the patronage of so great
a name. At the same time, there are not
wanting some who maintain that Cyprian
never held the opinion ascribed to him, but
that this was simply a forgery committed by
liars in his name.''

Proceeding with his introduction Dr. Coxe
tells us that the ''specialties'' of the Anglican Reformation were due to the writings of
Tertullian and Cyprian. The ''specialty'' of
the English Rebellion against the authority
of the Apostolic Chair, was a divorce case
of a particularly shocking character, and all
the special pleading and poisoning the wells
of history, that are possible, will never eliminate or obscure that fact. Nothing was far-
ther from the minds of the ecclesiastical con-
temporaries of Henry VIII, at the initial
stage of his struggle with Rome, than the
thought of building up a theological defense

of Henry's breach of the unity of the Church upon Tertullian and Cyprian as bases. The wretched time-servers who wore the livery of religion at that ill-starred period, were not so much concerned with the theological aspect of the case, as they were industrious to pander to the lusts of the royal brute, and thereby save their unworthy heads. It is not amazing that scholars devoted to the defense of Anglicanism should endeavor to make their case doctrinally and historically respectable; but it is surely astonishing, that in the face of so much history, men of intellectual credit, should endeavor to fabricate a case such as Dr. Coxe would have us accept. Perhaps the best refutation of Dr. Coxe's theory as to the "specialties" of the English Reformation (so miscalled), is seen in the thoroughly Papal character of Christianity in England, upon the eve of her great apostasy. The following words from a work entitled "Pilgrimage of Perfection" published in 1531, and said by the author William Bond a priest, to be profitable to all Christian persons to read, are not very suggestive of the "specialties" mentioned above. "There may be set no other foundation for the Church, but only that which is put, namely, Jesus Christ. It is certain, since it

is founded on the Apostles, as our Lord said
to Peter, 'I have prayed that thy faith fail
not.' And no more it shall; (for as St. Cyprian says), the Church of Rome was never
yet the root of heresy. This Church Apostolic is so named the Church of Rome, because St. Peter and St. Paul, who under God
were heads and princes of this Church, de-
posited there the tabernacles of their bodies,
which God willed should be buried there and
rest in Rome, and that should be the chief
see in the world; just as commonly in all
other places the chief see of the bishop, is
where the chief saint and bishop of the see
is buried. By this you may know, that Christ
is the head of the Church, and our Holy
Father the Pope is Head of the Church.
Many, because they know not this mystery of
Holy Scripture, have erred and fallen into
heresies, in denying the excellent dignity of
our Holy Father the Pope of Rome." [1]
Roger Edgeworth, a noted preacher in the
time of Henry VIII, speaking on the text:
"Tu vocaberis Cephas," says: "There
are as well texts of Holy Scripture and pas-
sages of ancient writers, which *abundantly*
prove the primacy of the Pope." [2] It would

[1] Quoted by Dom Gasquet. Eve of Reformation, pp. 74,
75.
[2] Ibid., p. 75.

be perfectly idle to contend that the preacher makes reference only to a primacy of honor, —a favorite expression with Anglicans—for the preacher, as is thoroughly clear from the context, discusses *that primacy then acknowledged in England,* namely one of jurisdiction. We have another magnificent testimony from the pen of William Powell, who wrote a work on the supremacy of the Pope, just after Henry VIII had published his famous "Assertio Septem Sacramentorum." Powell's book was published by Pynson in London in 1523. Its title runs: "Propugnaculum Summi Sacerdotii, etc., contra M. Lutherum." Powell assures his readers, that he had submitted his work to the most erudite authority at Oxford (eruditissimo Oxoniensium) before committing it to the printer's hands. Whatever else may have occupied Powell's mind, we may be perfectly sure that he was never a bit conscious of Dr. Coxe's "specialty" theory.

We shall in due time allow Cyprian to speak for himself, with a view to discovering any sympathy he may have had for such a movement as the English Reformation; but now we must devote a little space to Tertullian. Speaking of the Apostles as the divinely appointed transmitters of Christ's teaching he asks: "Was anything withheld from the knowledge of Peter, who is called 'the rock upon which the Church should be built'; who received 'the keys of the kingdom of heaven,' with the authority 'to bind and loose in heaven and upon earth '?'"[1] Again "He" (Paul), "as he himself narrates, went up to Jerusalem for the purpose of seeing Peter, because of his office no doubt, etc."[2] Again "Though you think that heaven is still closed, forget not that the Lord left here to Peter, *and through him* to the Church, the keys of it."[3] Dr. Coxe together with a number of his coreligionists allows special prerogatives to Peter (though just what these prerogatives were it is difficult to discover), but deny them to his successors. Coxe maintains that this view coincides with Tertullian's. Audiatur Tertullianus:—"Come now, you who would indulge a better curiosity, if you would apply it to the business of your salvation, enumerate the apostolic churches, in which the very chairs of the apostles are still pre-eminent in their places (suis locis praesident). . . . Achaia is very near (there you find Corinth). Since

[1] Contra Haereticos. Cap. XXII.
[2] Ibid., XXIII.
[3] Scarpiace X.

you are not very distant from Macedonia
you have Philippi: there also are the Thessa-
lonians. Since you are able to go over to
Asia you reach Ephesus. Since you are
near to Italy you have Rome from which
comes to us the very authority of the apostles
themselves. O, happy that Church into which
the apostles poured all their doctrine together with their blood; where Peter suffers
a passion like his Lord's; where Paul wins
a crown, etc."[1] Why does Tertullian accen-
tuate the fact that from Rome comes to us
the authority of the Apostles? The Catholic
Church alone furnishes an answer to this
query. "Pontifex maximus, episcopus episcoporum,"[2] are the terms which he applies
to the incumbent of the Roman See.
Why? Dr. Coxe says to express irony.
It is true that he is severely criticising the
Roman Pontiff for his decree concerning the
readmission of certain penitents to communion. But in this Victor or his successor was
not singular. The context does not allow Dr.
Coxe's interpretation. Tertullian by these
expressions simply designated the Pope as
the Head of the Church and therefore the
chief bishop of Christendom. What Tertul-

[1] Contra Haereticos XXXVI.
[2] De Modestia. Cap. I.

lian criticised in Victor (or his successor)
he might have criticised just as readily in any
orthodox bishop in the Catholic Church. The
merest tyro in Ecclesiastical History knows,
that decrees concerning the absolution of
penitents were by no means confined to the
promulgations of the bishops of Rome.
Bishop Coxe allows in this connection that
Victor (or his successor) seemed ambitious
of superiority over other bishops. This admission is I think equivalent to saying that
he was, to a degree, infected with popery.

The above excerpts from the ipsissima
verba of Tertullian though brief would at the
present day form sufficient ground for supposing that he had Papal leanings. Far from
forming the "specialty" of the English Reformers, the Catholic writings of Tertullian
would have been dangerous for the heads of
their advocates. The insistence upon the
Petrine prerogatives, and the maintenance of
the pre-eminence of the Roman See as set
forth by Tertullian, would have been ex-
tremely risky in England, while the erstwhile
Defender of the Seven Sacraments was "re-
forming" the Church there.

II

Speaking of Origen's frequent use of the
expression: "The Teaching of the Church,"
Dr. Coxe says: "It is noteworthy how often
our author uses this expression. . . . He
asserts 'a clearly defined teaching.' He
shows what the Church's teaching 'has laid
down.' He speaks of 'the faith of the
Church' and this as something accepted by all
Christians, recognized as orthodox or Catholics." [1] The admiration of Dr. Coxe for 'the
well defined teaching,' 'the dogmatic laying
down' and the recognized system of theological science, is curious, since in that sect of
which he was a member there is so little that
is definite in theology, and so much latitude is
allowed (or assumed) for divergency of doctrine. A writer who can hardly be accused
of bias, in his study of Anglicanism, very
truly says: "It is very difficult to expound
the doctrines of the Church of England. In
its three parties, it contains the three forms,
under which Christianity exists in the world
elsewhere in separate sects. The High
Church, which is now predominant represents
the Church idea, and is essentially to be
ranked with the Roman and Greek Churches.

[1] Ante-Nic. F.   Vol. IV, p. 382.

The Low Church, which has shrunk very much in numbers and influence, represents the Scriptural idea, and is essentially Protestant. The Broad Church is really rationalistic, and ranks with the liberal sects."[1] The ranking of even the High Church with the Catholic Church is only of a very qualified sort to be sure, but with this modification the author's words are literally true. And be it well remembered these various forms constitute *one communion*. The idea of associating definite teaching and dogmatic utterances of an authoritative character, with such a church is little short of preposterous. These words do not overstate the case a jot or a tittle, and hence it is that so many earnest scholars have found it impossible to keep their footing in the English Church. Bishop Coxe before attempting to show that Anglicanism and ante-Nicene Christianity are one, should have essayed the task (difficult enough God knows) of telling us just what Anglicanism is. It is exactly because of the value of those expressions in Origen, which aroused the admiration of Dr. Coxe, that "there is an utter incongruity (to use Newman's words) between Protestantism and historical Christianity, whether the latter be re-

[1] Lyon, Study of the Sects.   p. 88.

garded in the earlier or later centuries.
Protestantism can as little bear its ante-Nicene as its post-Tridentine period."[1] Con-
tinuing his elucidations on Origen, Dr. Coxe
emphasizes the prominence of Alexandria as
the great stronghold of orthodoxy—hinting
that the faith of the Church received its authoritative expression, before the Council of
Nice, in the Egyptian metropolis. "Is it not
clear," says Dr. Coxe, "that the West merely
responded Amen to what Alexandria had
taught from the beginning? Is not the evidence overwhelming that nothing but passive
testimony was thus far heard of in connection
with the see of Rome? If the 'teaching of
the Church,' then, was so far independent of
that see that Christendom neither waited for
its voice, nor recognized it as of any exceptional importance in the definition of the faith
and the elimination of heresy, is it not evident that the entire fabric of the Middle Age
polity in the West has its origin in times and
manners widely differing from the Apostolic
Age and that of the ante-Nicene Fathers?"[2]

I may state after the most unqualified fash-
ion, and without the slightest fear of success-

[1] Newman, Development of Christian Doctrines. Introduc., p. 8.
[2] Ante-Nicene Fathers. Vol. IV, p. 382.

ful contradiction, that Rome *never* responded to any doctrinal teaching proceeding from Alexandria. Dr. Coxe's statement is a plain (and to the student of Church history) unmistakable lie. It is an amazing lie (unlike most others) because there is not the merest shred of historical evidence to give it even an apparent support. Was it "only passive testimony" that was heard from Rome when Dionysius the Great Patriarch of Alexandria—that much vaunted stronghold of orthodoxy—was called to account by Dionysius, Bishop of Rome, when the former was suspected of heretical leanings? Far from asserting the superiority or even the equality of his see, when compared with that into which, as Tertullian said: "the Apostles poured all their doctrine together with their blood," Dionysius of Alexandria makes ample apology and defense to his namesake in Rome. Let us turn to St. Athanasius for an account of the episode. "A charge had been laid before the Bishop of Rome against the Bishop of Alexandria, as if he had said that the Son was made, etc. . . . The synod at Rome being indignant, Dionysius wrote to his namesake. The latter in defense wrote a book entitled 'Refutation and Defense.'" "My letter, as I said before," writes Dionysius of Alexandria to Dionysius of Rome, "owing to present circumstances, I am unable to produce, or *I should have sent you the very words I used,* or rather a copy of it all; which if I have a chance I still will do."[1]   If the teaching of the Church was so far independent of the Roman See, that Christendom neither waited for its voice nor recognized it of any exceptional importance, then what meaning shall we attach to the words of Socrates the historian, who tells us that "the churches are commanded by an ecclesiastical law to enact no ordinances against the mind of the bishop of Rome."[2]   Zozomen puts the matter even more strongly. This historian quotes Pope Julius as stating to the Eusebians at Antioch that "there is a sacerdotal law, which declares that whatever is determined against the judgment of the bishop of Rome is null and void."[3]   Let it be well remembered that both Zozomen and Socrates are writing events which took place after Nice and before Sardica; and as the canon above mentioned is not found among the commonly received twenty of Nice, it is only fair to conclude the Ante-nicene char-

1 Athan.   De Synodis. Conc. Armin. et Seleuc. III, 43.
2 Hist. Eccl. lib. II, C. VIII.
3 Hist. Eccl. lib. III, C. X.

acter of the enactment. And if the existence of a definite written law in the case is called into question, then the testimony of the two historians above mentioned is all sufficient to prove a generally acknowledged supremacy of Rome, the more so, since neither Socrates nor Zozomen faintly suggest that there was any controversy concerning the acknowledgment itself.

It will not be amiss to introduce here a reminder that a greater incumbent of the Alexandrian See than Dionysius, appealed to the central authority at Rome when he was deprived of his ecclesiastical rights, namely St. Athanasius. The account of that appeal by Socrates is all the more to our purpose since it includes the appeals of other bishops. "Athanasius, after a lengthened journey, at last reached Italy. . . . At the same time also Paul, bishop of Constantinople, Asclepas of Gaza, Marcellus of Ancyra and Lucius of Adrianople, having been accused on various charges, and expelled from their various churches arrived at the imperial city. There each laid his case before Julius the bishop of Rome. He on his part, *by reason of the Church of Rome's special privilege, sent them back again into the East, fortifying them with commendatory letters; and at the*

same time restored to each his own place,
and sharply rebuked those by whom they had
been deposed. Relying upon the signature
of Bishop Julius the bishops departed from
Rome and again took possession of their own
churches.'' [1] Julius himself writing to the
Eusebians at Antioch, declares that in
their synod with out both notifying and in-
viting him, they had neglected to observe the
Apostolic Canons.[2] Moreover he sets forth
most clearly the ancient prerogative of his
see. ''Why was nothing said to us concerning the Church of the Alexandrians in particular? Are you ignorant that the custom has
been for word to be sent first to us, and then
for a just decision to be sent from this place?
If then any suspicion rested upon the bishop
there, notice thereof ought to have been sent
to the Church of this place. . . . What
we have received from the holy Apostle Peter, that I indicate to you.''[3] The contention
that the Council of Sardica conferred upon
the Roman bishop the prerogative which Julius exercised is utterly untenable, since the
letter of Julius from which we have quoted is
ascribed by no authority to a date later than

[1] Soc. Hist. Eccl. lib. II, C. 15.
[2] Athan. Apol. Cont. Arian. Cap. II, 21.
[3] Athan. Apol. Contra Arian II, 35.

340 A. D., whereas the Council of Sardica
convened not earlier than 343 A. D. Some
place it as late as 347 A. D. Again it would
have been ridiculous for Pope Julius to have
quoted "a custom," under the circumstances,
unless that custom was well known and generally acknowledged. It is significant that
though the bishops gathered together at Antioch, considered that Julius had treated them
with scant courtesy, we have no record of
their having disputed his claims.

Having refreshed his soul with this burst
of enthusiasm for the imaginary pre-eminence
of Alexandria, Dr. Coxe, who is now bunch-
ing his hits (if I may dare so express my-
self), tells us that at the Second Ecumenical Council A. D. 381 Jerusalem is called
the mother of all the churches. "So ignorant," says he, "were the Fathers of that
date, of any other 'Mother Church,' that they
address this very statement to the clergy of
Rome." [1] It is perfectly true that in the
Synodal Epistle of the Second Ecumenical
Council which was held at Constantinople, we
find Jerusalem called the mother of all the
churches. That the Fathers wrote this simply from a chronological view-point is evi-
denced from the facts, that Constantinople is

[1] Ante-Nic. F. IV, p. 383.

mentioned before Jerusalem, and the Syrian
Church is named "the most ancient and truly
apostolic." The same Synodal Letter is addressed to Pope Damasus and his colleagues
at Rome. It is redolent of reverence and
regard for the occupant of the see of Rome,
and is largely apologetic for the Fathers of
Constantinople not having been able to accept the invitation extended to them by Damasus, to go to Rome and partake in the
deliberations of a synod held there. In order
to arrive at a fuller understanding of their
attitude toward the Apostolic See, we must
read part of the answer of Pope Damasus to
the bishops assembled at the Byzantine Capital. I do not see the necessity of quoting
from the Synodal Letter since it largely em-
bodies the creed of the Council, and is aimed
at the heresies of Arius, Sabellius, Paul of
Samosata, Apollinarius and others. The following extract is from the answer of Damasus: "Most honorable sons: Since your love
renders to the Apostolic See the reverence
which is owing to it; you exhibit it in no small
measure to ourselves. For even though in
the holy church in which the holy apostle sat [1]

[1] The peculiar construction of the Greek text of this
sentence leaves the latter part of it difficult to render into
English. I follow the translation made into Latin by
Valesius.

and taught us how to manage the helm which has been given to our care, we notwithstanding, confess that we are not worthy of the honor. . . . Remain on solid ground firm and steady in your faith, and for the future allow neither your clergy nor people to give ear to vain words and useless questions; for we have already given a form that he who declares himself a Christian may preserve it. . . . Here by the judgment of the Apostolic See in the presence of Peter the bishop of Alexandria, was Timotheus together with his teacher Apollinarius condemned. . . . May God keep you sound, most honored sons."[1] Is it not curious from the viewpoint of Dr. Coxe, that the Fathers of the Council did not take exception to the lofty tone of Damasus? The more especially since he calls the bishops assembled at Constantinople his "sons."

[1] Theodoret, lib. V. Cap. X.

CHAPTER IV

HIPPOLYTUS

Dr. Coxe tells us, in his introduction to the fifth volume of the Fathers, that St. Hippolytus shows us "to what a state of feebleness and humiliation the Roman Church had been brought, probably by neglect of preaching"; and that "Hippolytus had resisted Roman bishops as heretics." [1] The learned Doctor further informs us in his elucidation of Hippolytus, "that after the Council of Nice the Bishops of Rome were recognized as patriarchs, though equals among brethren, and nothing more." [2]

Respecting the precious bit of information vouchsafed above regarding the degraded condition of the Roman Church in the day of Hippolytus, it must be noted that the "Refutation of All Heresies," the work in which we find an energetic attack upon Popes Zephyrinus and Callistus, though ascribed to Hippolytus is not unquestionably one of his

[1] Ante-Nic. F. Vol. V, preface.
[2] Ante-Nic. F. Vol. V, p. 155.

45

productions. Its title is not found in-scribed upon the statue of Hippolytus un-earthed near the Church of San Lorenzo in Rome A. D. 1551. This monument repre-sents Hippolytus in a sitting posture, and upon the cathedra, we find a list of the Saint's writings. I may add here, that the identity of Hippolytus himself is far from definitely settled. He is traditionally known as the bishop of Portus near Rome; and though the tradition rests on a respectable foundation, it is not above suspicion. Eusebius mentions him in connection with Beryllus bishop of Bostra in Arabia, and says that he "pre-sided over another church," [1] but adds not a syllable of further information, save an enu-meration of his works. Eusebius however ascribes the work against all the heresies "πρὸς ἁπάσας τὰς αἱρέσεις" to Hippolytus.[2] Döl-linger gives him the altogether questionable distinction of being the first anti-pope. Now granting for the moment, that the "Refu-tation of All Heresies" is a genuine work of Hippolytus, and that he was a bishop of the Roman province, it would follow that he was a schismatic, since we have not a single shred of historical testimony im-

[1] Euseb. Hist. Eccl. VI, 20.
[2] Euseb. Ibid., VI, 23.

pugning Zephyrinus and Callistus *as bishops
of Rome*. Moreover no historian or Ante-
nicene writer save himself, gives Callistus
an evil reputation. Both East and West are
perfectly silent on the ecclesiastical difficulties of the Roman See of the period *as they
are set forth by Hippolytus*. The following
appreciation of the case from the pen of the
learned Dr. McGiffert, himself an Anglican,
is I think as fair a view of the subject as one
could wish for. ''The schism which has left
no trace in the writings of either the Western
or Eastern Church, cannot have been a serious one. Doubtless Callistus had the support of by far the larger portion of the
Church, and the opposition of Hippolytus
never amounted to anything more than talk,
and was never strong enough to enlist or
perhaps even attempt to enlist the support
of foreign bishops. Callistus and the body
of the Church could afford to leave it unno-
ticed; and after Callistus' death, Hippolytus
undoubtedly returned to the Church, and was
gladly received, and the memory of his brief
schism entirely effaced.'' [1] Dr. Coxe makes
a great demonstration against what he deli-
cately terms ''the Papal imposture'' with St.

[1] Euseb. Hist. Eccl. VI, 23 note. (Transl. by Dr. Ar-
thur McGiffert.)

Hippolytus as his chief support. He promises to repair the "infinite damage done to history" and "to restore scientific precision" in the appreciation of the position of the bishop of Rome. We have a right to expect great things from him. He disappoints us however, and reminds one of lines which always appeal to the humorous sense of a college lad:

"Quid dignum tanto feret hic promissor hiatu?
Parturiunt montes, nascetur ridiculus mus."

Rome did not have to wait for the august assembly at Nice to give her a position of honor and jurisdiction—not a mere precedence; but after the famous council, Rome's position shone out in a clearer and more unmistakable light. Dr. Coxe's statement therefore, concerning the position of the ante-Nicene popes as "mere bishops," and their post-Nicene patriarchal dignity unaccompanied with any special jurisdiction, is not only in contradiction to known history, but is an expression of both ignorant and much-inflamed prejudice. We find in the Arabic canons attributed to the First Council of Nice the following decree (Canon xxxix of the series): "The patriarch must con-

sider what things are done by the archbishops and bishops in their provinces; and
should he find things otherwise than is meet
and proper, he should change and dispose
matters as he shall deem proper, for they
(the bishops) are his sons and he is the
father of all, . . . just as he who occu-
pies the chair of Rome, is the head and prince
of all patriarchs; since he is the first, as was
Peter, to whom power is given over all Christian princes, and over all their peoples, as
he who is the Vicar of Christ our Lord, over
all peoples and over the whole Christian
Church, and whoever shall gainsay this is
excommunicated by the Synod." [1]   I am perfectly aware that there has been a very long
and as yet unsettled controversy, as to the
exact number of canons promulgated by the
Council of Nice. I am aware also that *perhaps* the more critical view seems to point to
only twenty canons, whereas the Arabic man-
uscript translated into Latin by Father Romanus S. J. points to eighty. The antiquity of the Arabic MS. however is not to
be called into question, and the fact that it
proceeds from an oriental source, makes it
valuable in this connection. Abraham Echel-

[1] Labbe & Cossart Concilia. Tom. II, Coll. 291 — Transl.
by Romanus, S.J.

lensis, a scholarly Maronite, made a profound study of the Arabic canons and in
1645, published a Latin translation of them.
His arrangement differs somewhat from that
of Father Romanus the erudite Jesuit, who
made his translation from a Vatican MS.,
which was bought for it probably by the
famous Asseman from the Coptic Patriarch
John. The following is a translation from
the Latin of Abraham Echellensis (Canón
xxxvii of his collection). "There shall be
only four patriarchs in the whole world, just
as there were four writers of the Gospel.
. . . And there shall be over them as head
and prince, the lord of the see of the Divine
Peter at Rome, according as was commanded
by the Apostles." The Council of Sardica
was held probably in 344, certainly not later
than 347. Its canons were accepted by the
Greeks as ecumenical, and are by them still
so regarded. The fourth canon of said council is as follows (from the Greek): "Bishop
Gaudentius said: If it appears well to you,
it behooves us to add to this enactment full
of unquestionable love, which thou hast pronounced, that, if any bishop be deprived of
his seat by the judgment of (these) neighbor-
ing bishops, and set forth that he has new
cause in defense, a new bishop shall not be

established in his see, unless the bishop of
Rome judge and render a decision as to this.''
Canon third of this same council is the same
proposition addressed to the Fathers of Sardica by the president of the council, Hosius.
Canon fifth is simply a conciliar ratification
of the same. The contention that Sardica
granted to Rome what she did not possess
before is groundless. The history of appeals to Rome in the ante-Nicene period
proves this, as do also the facts that Athanasius of Alexandria and Paul of Constantinople together with other bishops as we
have seen above, appealed to Rome before
the Council of Sardica was convened, and
were restored to their respective sees by the
authority of the *Pope*.

It is difficult to see how Dr. Coxe has the
temerity to state, that after the Council of
Nice the Roman patriarch was regarded as
an equal among brethren. He tells us that
Gregory the Great had little patience with
such a title as ''universal bishop,'' and that
the same blessed Pope looked upon its assumption as an expression of ''intolerable
pride.'' This is perfectly true, but that the
same Gregory was thoroughly imbued with
the correct notion of his own high office, as
bishop of Rome none who know aught of his

history will presume to deny. No Pope as-
sumes the title of "universal bishop." The
Papacy cannot annul the episcopate, which
is equally of divine origin. The rights and
prerogatives of the other Apostles are not
sacrificed upon the altar of Peter's honor and
jurisdiction. This was the idea of the great
St. Gregory. His own words are the best
testimony as to how he looked upon the See
of the Fisherman. In his epistle to John
Bishop of Syracuse, St. Gregory says, "The
Byzantine primate had been accused on some
charge, and the most pious Emperor wished
him to be *judged by us,* according to canonical
ordinance. . . . As to his saying that he
is subject to the Apostolic See; if any fault is
found in bishops, *I know not what bishop is
not subject to it."* [1] No mediæval Pope ever
said more than this. Whatever Gregory's
views were as to the title of "universal
bishop," he certainly never favored any minimizing of the prerogative of his see. Dr.
Coxe informs us in this connection that Nicholas I (A. D. 858) was the first "pope" in
the "Tridentine sense." Herein Coxe has
the merit of unquestionable originality, and
Nicholas was bravely progressive—just
about nine hundred years ahead of his time.

[1] Greg. Ep. LIX.

Dr. Coxe is angry nearly always, but occasionally (though unconsciously) he will inject a drop of humor into his wrathful work. Can the reader imagine the creation of the papal power three hundred years after Leo had hurled back to Chalcedon the famous twenty-eighth canon; three hundred years after the Fathers of Chalcedon had cried out, "Peter hath spoken through Leo."

In his tenth elucidation of Hippolytus Dr. Coxe tells us, that the Vatican definition of Papal Infallibility clothes the "errors of Callistus and Zephyrinus with infallibility." [1] As there is no historical evidence of an unquestionable character, that either of the above named popes ever taught anything subversive to either faith or morals, and as it is certain that neither of them *defined* anything, we need waste no time in further disposing of Dr. Coxe's statement. This is not the place to discuss the personal record of Callistus before he became an ecclesiastic. From the account given by Hippolytus (on the assumption that the "Refutation of All Heresies" is a genuine work of the saint), Callistus was a very interesting sinner before conversion; but we have seen that Hippolytus himself was not above suspicion. Dr.

[1] Vol. V, p. 158.

Wordsworth's "St. Hippolytus and the See of Rome," a work upon which Dr. Coxe so heavily leaned, is a book of most patent bias and misreading of history. The author creates out of the "Refutation of All Heresies" and the abundance of his own prejudices, a structure against the Papacy, as flimsy as the unsubstantial fabric of a dream. It may not be out of place here to observe that Dr. Coxe is wont to speak so feelingly of the "Great Eastern Church." Does he imagine for a moment, that the schismatical churches of the East regard his communion in any light save that of an heretical sect? Is he alive to the doctrinal teaching of the Orient regarding the Seven Sacraments, the Sacrifice of the Mass, the practice of Confession, devotion to the Blessed Mother of God, and the Saints, the veneration of holy relics and sacred images, and the profession of monastic vows? Where in God's name is the foundation of the professed sympathy of Englishmen for the Greek Church, which turns from England's approaches with cold disregard, and shows her practical view of Anglican pretensions by refusing to regard as valid ministrations, the pseudo-sacramental acts of her clergy. Most of my readers are familiar with the details of a case very much in point in which a recent convert from the ranks of the Episcopal ministry, was rebaptized and reordained by a Russian bishop.[1]

There is a very large consolation, however, in contemplating the fact, that England is not without a real hierarchy and a valid priesthood. Where heresy and persecution of the elect reigned supreme, again is offered the "Clean Oblation"; again the faithful kneel at the feet of God's minister in that "little house of grief," to find remission of their sins; again the psalmody is heard in cloistered choirs; and again the staff of Christendom's White Shepherd is acknowledged—for God is more truly known. "Canterbury has gone its way, and York is gone, and Durham is gone, and Winchester is gone. It was sore to part with them. We clung to the vision of past greatness, and would not believe it could come to naught; but the Church in England has died, and the Church lives again. Westminster and Nottingham, Beverly and Hexham, Northhampton and Shrewsbury, if the world lasts, shall be names as musical to the ear, as stirring to the heart, as the glories we have lost; and Saints shall rise out of them, if God so will, and Doctors

[1] The case of Dr. Irvine.

shall once again give the law to Israel, and
Preachers call to penance and to justice, as
at the beginning.'' [1]

Before taking leave of Dr. Coxe's elucidations on St. Hippolytus we must notice a
footnote found among them which runs as
follows: ''In England the (Papal) 'supremacy' was never acknowledged, nor in France
till now.'' [2] The reference to France may
be dismissed without notice, since it merits
none. The brazen effrontery of such a declaration is its best commentary. With respect to England's acknowledgment of the
supremacy of the Roman See, we are able to
bring forth striking testimonies. We can
hardly do better than follow here the guidance of the erudite Abbot Gasquet.[3] Having
for his object the proper definition of the
Pope's position in England on the eve of the
Reformation, Dom Gasquet says, ''We, nat-
urally turn to the works of Sir Thomas
More for evidence of the teaching as to the
Pope's position at this period; and his testimony is both abundant and definite. Thus in
the second book of his ''Dyalogue,'' written

[1] Sermons on Various Occasions. "The Second Spring."
—Newman.
[2] Vol. V, 155.
[3] "On the Eve of the Reformation," pp. 77 *et seq.*

in 1528, arguing that there must be unity in the Church of Christ, he points out that the effect of Lutheranism, has been to breed diversity of faith and practice. ''Though they began so late,'' he writes, ''yet there are not only as many sects almost as men, but also the masters themselves change their minds and opinions every day. Bohemia is also in the same case; one faith in the town, another in the field; one in Prague, another in the next town; and yet in Prague itself, one faith in one street, another in the next. And yet all these acknowledge that they cannot have the Sacraments ministered, but by such priests as are made by the authority derived and conveyed from the Pope, who is, under Christ, Vicar and head of our Church.'' [1] ''The Church has begun with Christ, and has had Him for its head, and St. Peter His Vicar after Him, and the head under Him; and always since the successors of him continually.'' [2] We find the following extract in a sermon preached at a synod of archbishops and bishops held at Westminster in 1527. The discourse is directed against the errors of Luther, and incidentally touches upon the

[1] English Works, p. 171.
[2] Ibid., p. 185.

affliction brought upon the pope by Luther's rebellion. Bishop Longland is the preacher. "Shall we not mourn," he cries, "for the evil life of the chief Church (of Christendom)? Shall we not beseech God for the liberation of the primate and chief ruler of the Church? Let us pray then; let us pray that through our prayers we may be heard. Let us implore freedom for our mother, the Catholic Church, and the liberty, so necessary for the Christian religion, of our chief Father on earth—the Pope." [1]

When Dr. John Clark, the English ambassador in Rome, presented to Leo X in open consistory the famous "Assertio Septem Sacramentorum" of Henry VIII, he said, "that in the mind of his sovereign the attack on the Pope by Luther was an attack upon a divinely established order." He protested in the name of Henry, "the devotion and veneration of the king toward the Pope and his most Holy See." "Luther had declared war," said the minister, "not only against your Holiness, but also against your office, . . . and against that Rock, established by God Himself." "England," continued the speaker, "has never been behind other nations, in the worship of God and the

[1] Joannis Longlondi Tres Conciones (R. Pynson). f. 45.

Christian faith, and in obedience to the Roman Church."[1]

Such testimonies as the above leave no doubt in a fair mind as to the relation between the Holy See and England in prereformation times; and they prove that Bishop Coxe was either ignorant of a great deal of history, or unscrupulous in his dealing with it.

[1] Assertion of the Seven Sacraments against Luther (Transl. by J. W., 1687), f. a. i.

CHAPTER V

ST. CYPRIAN

For the sake of convenient arrangement, I have thought it fitting, to order in a set of propositions Dr. Coxe's introduction to the works of St. Cyprian, and then to refute them separately. Dr. Coxe clearly felt the difficulty of handling the case of Cyprian and the Holy See, but being a man inseparably wedded to his errors, essentially Protestant, and incorrigibly anti-Roman he bravely faces the task, with what result we shall shortly see. His introduction to Cyprian may be aptly summed up in the following statements:

1. Nothing can be more delusive than the idea, that "the mediæval system derives any support from Cyprian's theory of the episcopate or Church organization. His was the system of universal parity of bishops."

2. The "terrible schism of the ninth century," placed the Latin Churches upon the foundation of the "Forged Decretals."

3. The primacy of which Cyprian was an

early promoter, had to be entirely destroyed by decretalism, before the Papacy could exist. Gregory the Great stood upon the Cyprianic base, when he pronounced the author of a scheme for a "universal bishopric" to be a "forerunner of Antichrist."

4. If the adherents of American Romanism ever "fully understand this great Carthaginian Father," a "glorious reformation of this alien religion," will be the result.

We can readily afford to ignore the insult which the words "mediæval system" thinly veil. There is too much resplendent testimony in the history of the first six centuries of our era, in favor of the Papacy for us to bother about the hard sayings of a man who (apparently at least), has endeavored persistently to close his eyes to the light. The best refutation of Dr. Coxe's first proposition, is found in the words of Cyprian himself. Let the ancient saint and martyr speak then—we shall listen and then judge.

Pope Cornelius complained that he was ignored in the matter of sending him information about troublous affairs at Adrumetum— the peace of the Church having been disturbed there. Cyprian, who with other bishops, and a number of presbyters, had gathered at Adrumetum to remedy the difficulties, on becom-

ing aware of Cornelius' displeasure, wrote
him an apologetic letter. The following extracts from the same need no commentary.
"Cyprian to Cornelius, etc. . . . I have
read your letters, dearest brother, . . .
in which I saw that you were annoyed."
(Because he had not been furnished with the
aforesaid information.) "In respect to which
I desire you to know and certainly to believe,
that it was not done from any thought-
lessness or disrespect." . . . "We fur-
nish every person who sails from here to you
with directions that they may sail without
giving offense. We have insisted with them,
I would have you know, that they acknowledge and hold fast to the *root* and *matrix* of
the Church Catholic. . . . Lest a schism
made in the city, should confuse the minds
of the absent with uncertain opinions, we de-
cided . . . that letters should be sent you
by all who were placed anywhere in the province, as in fact is done, so that all of our colleagues might both firmly approve and hold
to you and your communion, *that is to both
the unity* as well as the charity of the Catholic Church."[1] "Communicationem ejus, id
est *Catholicæ Ecclesiæ unitatem,* pariter et
caritatem probare ac tenere." "Rome,"

[1] Ep. XLIV ad Cornel.

says St. Cyprian, writing of the sees of Rome and Carthage respectively, "must take precedence of Carthage, by reason of her greatness.[1] In his letter to Antonianus concerning the case between Pope Cornelius and the heretic Novation, he says: "You wrote, moreover, for me to send a copy of those epistles to Cornelius our colleague, so that he might put away all worry, and know at once that you held communion *with him, that is with the Catholic Church*."[2] Further on in the same letter he states that a "large number of African bishops had gathered together after persecution, to discuss the question of readmitting the lapsed. "And lest, perhaps," says he, "the number of bishops in Africa might not seem sufficient (or satisfactory), we wrote to Rome, to Cornelius our colleague concerning this thing, etc." Why was it necessary or even expedient to write to Rome? Did not Cyprian believe in the universal parity of bishops? Why then was it proper or necessary to encourage a doubt as to the insufficiency of the "large number" of African bishops, and to settle that doubt by an appeal to Rome? St. Cyprian has an answer for us. It was because Cornelius had reached the "pinnacle (or summit) of the

[1] Ep. XLVII.
[2] Ep. LI.

priesthood,'' by reason of the fact that he held ''the place of Peter [1] and the grade of the sacerdotal throne.'' [2]   Cyprian's explanation of schism, found in another letter to the same Pope is very much ad rem: ''For neither have heresies arisen nor have schisms originated, from any other source, than from this, that God's priest is not obeyed; nor do they reflect that for the time being, there is one person who is priest in the Church, and for the time judge in the place of Christ, whom, if, according to the divine teaching, *all the faithful should obey,* no one would stir up anything against the congregation of priests, etc.'' [3]   Bishop Coxe explains this passage as referring to the supremacy of each bishop in his own see.[4]   Students of Church History are too well aware of the fact, that such a supremacy carries with it no guarantee against schism to be led captive by such an interpretation. The passage of Cyprian's letter to Pope Cornelius stands best without comment. ''Peter,'' he writes in that same document, ''upon whom by that same Lord the Church had been built, speaking *one for all*, and *answering with the voice of the Church,* says, Lord to whom shall we go?''

---

[1] Ep. LI.
[2] Ibid.
[3] Ep. LIV.
[4] Vol. V, p. 340.

Explaining to Cornelius why he had not written about Fortunatus the pseudo-bishop and his supporters, he says: "The matter was not such as ought immediately and with haste to be brought to your attention as if it were great or to be dreaded. . . . I did not think it necessary that the foolishness of heretics should be hastily and urgently brought before you. . . . It was determined upon by the judgment of us all to write to you, that a short way might be discovered of dissipating error and arriving at truth." [1] Toward the end of the same letter describing to Cornelius what he regards as the very acme of arrogance on the part of Fortunatus and his abettors, he writes, "After such things as these, they still dare—a spurious bishop having been elected for them by heretics—to set sail and carry letters from schismatics and profane persons to the chair of Peter, and to the principal church, whence sacerdotal unity has taken its rise, forgetting that these are the Romans whose faith the Apostle praised, and to whom faithlessness can have no access." "Navigare audent ad Petri cathedram et ad Ecclesiam principalem, unde unitas sacerdotalis exorta est; nec cogitare eos esse Romanos quorum fides Apostolo

[1] Ep. LIV.

prædicante laudata est, ad quos perfidia habere non possit accessum.'' [1]   I can readily fancy how poor Dr. Coxe's heart sank when he read Cyprian's fifty-fourth letter; and considering the task he had set for himself, I don't wonder a bit. I may remark incidentally that the heretics too knew of Rome's position, and the value of her patronage.

If Dr. Coxe's notion, that Cyprian held the universal parity of bishops, be true, is it not a bit curious, that Cyprian should request Pope Stephen to excommunicate Marcion the bishop of Arles? "You should send letters by which Marcion being excommunicated, etc." [2]   Making reference to Peter's humility anent the controversy between the Prince of the Apostles and Paul, Cyprian in a letter to Quintus a bishop in Mauretania writes: "For neither did Peter whom the Lord chose first, and upon whom He built His Church, when Paul argued with him about the circumcision, insolently claim anything to himself, nor proudly assume anything, so as to declare that he held the primacy." [3]

When Cyprian and his colleagues in Africa had held their famous council, to deliberate upon the re-baptism of heretics they sent the

[1] Ep. LIV.   [3] Ep. LXX.
[2] Ep. LXVI.

result of their sessions to Stephen for approval. There is no controversy upon this point. Stephen was clearly conscious of his power, as head of the Church, when he *condemned and annulled* their main proceeding with his well known "nil innovetur." Cyprian's rebellion against the papal act can never invalidate his manifold testimonies regarding the See of Rome, as the center of unity, the "root and matrix" of the Church, and the seat of universal jurisdiction. Firmillian Bishop of Cæsarea in Cappadocia, who sympathized with Cyprian in the controversy, furnishes us with valuable testimony as to an ante-Nicene pope's concept of his own position and authority. In a letter to Cyprian, Firmillian uses the following expressions: "Stephen who so brags of the place of *his bishopric,* insisting upon his succession from Peter on whom the foundations of the Church were laid, . . . Stephen who announces that he holds by succession the throne of Peter." "They who are at Rome . . . vainly arrogate to themselves the authority of the apostles." I fear that Stephen was very much of a Pope in the "Tridentine sense."

Were the above quotations from the works

1 Ep. Firm ad Cyp. in oper. Cyp. inventa LXXIV.

of St. Cyprian found in a work proceeding
from the Anglican source, I think it perfectly
safe to say that the author would be pronounced—and very promptly—infected with
"Romanism." I conclude from the aforesaid quotations, that Cyprian believed Peter
to be the Rock upon which Christ built His
Church; that his successors at Rome were
invested with a primacy not simply of honor
but of jurisdiction; and that only on the supposition of such an attitude toward Rome on
the part of Cyprian can we understand or
explain, his deference toward the Roman
bishop before the clash with Stephen, his re-
alization that the Pope should be apprized of
disorders existing no matter where in the
Church, his request that the bishop of Rome
should excommunicate another member of
the episcopate, and finally his sending the deliberations and decrees of a provincial council to Rome for Papal approval.

Thus the first proposition of Dr. Coxe is
irremediably damaged.

As to the second it is all sufficient to say
that the dreadful schism of the ninth century
could not have brought about the Pope's spiritual supremacy from the simple fact that the
Papal supremacy was an unquestionable fact
before the schism, and the schism itself was

an act of rebellion against Roman authority. The history of that lamentable episode of the Church's troubles, the letters of Pope Nicholas I, Photius and the Byzantine Emperors, Basil and Leo, all point out most clearly, a pre-existing acknowledgment of the prerogatives of the Apostolic See, the supremacy of which began to impress itself upon the life of the Church, when Clement of Rome took care of the schism at Corinth, and it continued with greater or less emphasis according to varying exigencies to make itself felt until our day.

The third proposition is easily met. The primacy which the unbiased reader finds in Cyprian, is founded upon two facts. First, that Peter was constituted the rock upon which the fabric of the Church is reared, and is therefore the first and chief apostle, and head of the Church in the matter of jurisdiction as well as in that of honor; second, that Peter's successors in the Roman See inherit his headship, that is, his jurisdiction and honor. Now as these are the essential features of the present Papal system, it follows cogently that the "primacy" which Cyprian supported should not be abolished, to make room for a later and different one. St. Cyprian's writings would need many and serious alterations to make him a witness for Anglicanism. Dr. Coxe labors hard with the various texts above cited, in order to minimize or explain them away. At times his efforts provoke a smile. He hammers away concerning the "Forged Decretals" at nearly every step, as though the Papacy was not a most firmly established and undisputed fact before that puzzling forgery was ever thought of. We shall notice in some detail further on, Dr. Coxe's insistence upon the dependence of the Papacy upon the "Decretals."

Regarding Dr. Coxe's hope for the conversion of "American Romanists," perhaps it suffices to say that the outlook from his point of view is somewhat depressing. I'm sure it must have discouraged him a bit. It is not marvelous, however, that he omits any reference to that constantly growing number of souls who are daily leaving the Protestant Episcopal Church for the light and warmth of Catholicism.

"Cyprian," says Dr. Coxe, "is often incorrectly quoted by Roman controvertists against the very principles of Cyprian himself, of his life and writings. This is due to the fact that they have in their hands vitiated and interpolated copies. Thus take the famous passage as follows; Cyprian: 'Loquitur Dominus ad Petrum, Ego tibi dico Tu es Petrus etc. (a) Super unum (b) ædificat ecclesiam. Hoc erant utique et caeteri apostoli quod fuit Petrus, qui consortio praediti et honoris et potestatis, sed exordium ab unitate proficiscitur (c) ut (d) Ecclesia (e) Dei una monstretur (f).

Qui Ecclesiae resistitur et resistit (g), in ecclesia se esse confidit?'

INTERPOLATED

(a) Et iterum eidem post resurrectionem suam dicit Pasce oves meas.

(b) Super illum unum . . . et illi pascendas mandat oves suas.

(c) Et Primatus datur Petro.

(d) Una.

(e) Et Cathedra.

(f) Et pastores sunt omnes et grex unus ostenditur, qui ab apostolis omnibus, unanimi consensione pascatur, etc.

(g) Qui cathedram Petri, super quem fundata est ecclesia deserit, etc.

"This is but a specimen," continues Dr. Coxe, "of the way in which Cyprian has been doctored. . . . Baluzius rejected these interpolations." [1]

It must be noted here that the most crit-

[1] Ante-Nic. F. Vol. V, p. 558.

ical edition of Cyprian is that of the famous Benedictine congregation of St. Maur.
Baluzius, the justly recognized patristic
scholar, who was a monk of this congregation, edited and annotated Cyprian's works.
The translations into English of these
works have been made in the light of the
labors of Baluzius. Needless to say I re-
fer to the renditions of Edinburgh and Oxford. The American edition is merely a reprint of the Oxford translation with the notes
of the egregious Coxe. Protestant scholars,
almost to a man, grant the eminently critical
character of the work of Baluzius. The following is the text of the "interpolated" passage, cited above, as I find it set forth by
Baluzius: "Probatio est ad fidem facilis,
compendio veritatis. Loquitur Dominus ad
Petrum 'Ego tibi dico,' 'inquit,' 'quia tu es
Petrus, etc.' . . . Super illum unum
ædificat ecclesiam suam, et illi pascendas
mandat oves suas. Et quamvis Apostolis
omnibus, post resurrectionem suam parem
potestatem tribuat et dicat: 'Sicut misit me
Pater, etc.' . . . tamen ut unitatem mani-
festaret, unam cathedram constituit. Hoc-
erant utique et ceteri Apostoli quod fuit Petrus, pari consortio praediti et honoris et potestatis: sed exordium ab unitate proficisci-

tur (et primatus Petro datur), ut una Christi Ecclesia, et cathedra, una monstretur." [1] Baluzius takes exception to the words which I have enclosed with parentheses. This phrase he looks upon as a marginal note, since it is not found in every codex. With the exception of this parenthesis the text stands as above in every codex and in every edition. The sputterings of Dr. Coxe, concerning the nameless monk,[2] who tampered with the notes of Baluzius are beneath the notice of a scholar. They are the merest gratuities, founded on no respectable evidence, and suggested by an edition of Cyprian's treatise "De Unitate," published under the supervision (or editorship) of Dr. Hyde, in Burlington, N. J. (A. D. 1852), a book filled with typographical errors and more serious blunders—a work in short of no critical value whatever. It is not remarkable that Coxe is enthusiastic over the work and sympathetic with its editor—similis simili gaudet. Throw aside the parenthesis; pare the passage down to the limits of Dr. Coxe (if so I may speak), and still it remains an unmistakable testimony of the Papal prerogatives.

[1] Cyp. De Unitate Eccl. C. IV. apud. Migne Patrol.
[2] Vol. V, 558.

CHAPTER VI

The eighth volume of the ante-Nicene series furnishes us with Dr. Coxe's most vigorous effort. It will require a great deal of
tactful care, to avoid referring again to what
has been sufficiently refuted already in these
pages. This care is rendered necessary by
the untiring repetitions of Dr. Coxe. He
never wearies of repeating again and again
the same bits of miserable sophistry, special
pleading and plain falsehood. One is almost
forced to the conclusion that the object he
had in view in editing the "Fathers," had
so taken hold of his mind as to have disor-
dered (at least in some degree) his faculties.
His zeal betrays him into fellowship with
every heretic and rebel against ecclesiastical
unity. Any bishop of the ante-Nicene period, who attempts to withstand Roman authority, is immediately taken to Coxe's
bosom, and becomes a hero in the cause of
the rights of the Episcopate. It would indeed be amusing were it not so distressing.

74

We shall now proceed to pick out of his eight
neatly set forth propositions (which he declares must be perfectly clear to students
who have read the ante-Nicene Fathers with
his notes), those which we regard it necessary to notice.   Dr. Coxe, in his second proposition contends "that it is a fundamental
fact, that the Apostolic Sees were all equally
accounted *matrices* of unity and the roots of
the other churches."   "Down to the Council
of Nicæa," he continues, "the whole system
of the Church was framed on this principle;
these were the ancient customs which the
council ordained to be perpetual. Because it
was the capital of the empire, and *for no
other reason* (the Petrine idea never once
mentioned), the primacy of honor was con-
ceded to Old Rome, and *equal* honor to New
Rome, because it was the new capital." [1]

If the foregoing statements be true then
the following testimonies presumably a trifle
more authoritative and respectable than Dr.
Coxe's, are utterly worthless. The reader
will pardon necessary repetitions.

1. Clement of Rome during the lifetime of
John the Evangelist, hearkens to an appeal
from Corinth, and issues an unmistakably
authoritative document which quieted the dis-

[1] Ante-Nicene F.   Vol. VIII, p. 602.

turbance then existing in the Corinthian Church. The letter was read in Corinth and elsewhere at public services for *several centuries*. 2. Ignatius of Antioch declares that the Roman Church rules over the Church (coetus caritatis), and holds the dignity of the first place. 3. Irenæus calls the Church of Rome—the greatest, with which all others must agree by reason of its great power. 4. "From Rome," says Tertullian, "comes to us the very authority of the Apostles themselves." "Pontifex maximus, episcopus episcoporum," are titles with which he designates the incumbent of the Roman See. 5. Cyprian identifies Rome with the Catholic Church. "He is in communion with Cornelius, that is with the Catholic Church." He maintains that the unity of the priesthood has its source in the Roman Church, and that "perfidia" can have no access to the Romans. He begs Rome to excommunicate a bishop. 6. Victor of Rome excommunicates the churches of Asia. 7. The Montanists from Phrygia take their cause to Rome. 8. Dionysius of Rome calls Dionysius of Alexandria to account for his teaching, and the Alexandrian bishop both submits and explains. 9. Stephen utterly refuses to treat with the emissaries of Cyprian, and annuls the main proceeding of the Carthaginian council.

If the foregoing ante-Nicene testimonies in favor of the ''Petrine idea'' as Dr. Coxe calls it, be valueless, what then in God's name constitutes historically reliable evidence? To contend that the ante-Nicene period of the Church's history speaks no word for the Papacy, is to give the lie to facts. To maintain that the doctrine of Papal supremacy did not express itself to the full in the ante-Nicene period, is not only legitimate, but unquestionably expedient. I am aware that some would have us believe that the same universal acknowledgment on the part of the Church, and the same active maintenance of power on the part of Peter's See has characterized the history of the Papacy from the days of the Apostles down to our own times. I am equally aware however that such a position is untenable, because irreconcilable with history, and it constitutes a most feeble defense of the Papacy itself. The illustrious Newman gave us a world of teaching on the matter, when he pointed out that the interpretation of the second and third centuries of our era, in their attitude towards Rome, is found in the fourth and fifth. And as our misguided friend Coxe plunges madly over the Nicene border, it is proper that we should follow him as far as our purpose demands.

"The mighty centralization about Constantinople;" he continues, "the three councils held within its walls; the virtual session of the other councils under its eaves; the inconsiderable figure of 'Old Rome' in strictly ecclesiastical history; her barrenness of literature, and of great heroic sons, . . . and her decadence as a capital, had led Leo I and others after him to dwell much upon 'St. Peter,' and to favor new ideas of his personal greatness, and of a transmitted grandeur as the inheritance of his successors. As yet these were but 'great swelling words of vanity;' but they led to the formulated fraud of the Decretals."[1] Bishop Coxe wrote the above in a hurry. It is a little difficult to see how the three councils held within the walls of the Byzantine capital could have formed any part of the inspiration of Leo I, to insist on the greatness of Peter and the See of Rome, since Leo was a long time dead before the Second Council of Constantinople was thought of. This was a bold stroke on the part of Dr. Coxe. In order to be well impressed with the "inconsiderable figure of

[1] Ante-Nic. F.   Vol. VIII, p. 662.

'Old Rome,' " in Leo's time, we must turn to that lofty-minded and vigorous character himself, for an account of his view.

It is still very early in the Church's history; but a hundred years, since the august gathering at Nicæa had formed the first great Christian synod. On September 29, A. D. 440, Leo, so deservedly called the great, ascended the throne of Peter. Not long after that event, and surely before he could have shaped a policy by which to compete with Constantinople, and while still in a measure, under the surprise which took possession of him, when the deputation from the Eternal City had informed him, then in Gaul on a political mision, that Sixtus had died and that he was chosen for Peter's chair, he spoke as follows in a sermon to the Roman people: "Divine mercy has made this a day of honor for me, for by raising my humbleness to the highest rank, it has made manifest, that He has not held in contempt any of His own. . . . I confess my joy over your devotion, when I behold this magnificent assemblage of my venerable brothers of the priesthood. . . . I feel sure, that the fostering interest and sincere love of the Apostle Peter is not wanting to this congregation: he has not despised your devotion in whose honor you are gathered together. . . . He rejoices in your respect for the Lord's own institution, *as shown toward the partners of his honor*. . . . In order therefore, dearly beloved, that this loyalty which you so unanimously show toward my littleness, may obtain the proper result of its ardor, on bended knee beg the condescending goodness of our God that he will . . . deign to render me his poor servant, whom to show the treasures of His grace He has willed to *place at the helm of His Church,* sufficient for so great a work." [1] We find in another sermon of Leo, delivered probably on the third anniversary of his accession a still stronger exposition of the "Petrine idea." "The dispensation of Truth still abides, and the blessed Peter persevering in the strength of the Rock, which he has received, has not abandoned the helm of the Church, which he undertook. For he was ordained in such wise before the rest, that from his being named the Rock, from his being declared the Foundation, from his being appointed the Gatekeeper of the kingdom of heaven, from his being placed as the Judge to bind and to loose, whose judgments shall remain valid in heaven, from all these mystical appellations,

[1] Sermon I.

we might realize the nature of his relation-
ship with Christ. And to-day, he does the
work committed to him, thoroughly and ef-
fectually, and performs every portion of his
duty and mission in Him, and with Him,
through Whom he has been glorified. And
hence if anything is properly done and justly
decreed by us, if anything is obtained from
God's mercy by our daily prayers, it is of
his work and merits *whose power lives, and
whose authority prevails in his See.*" [1]   One
would almost believe that Leo had a copy of
the "Forged Decretals," in his inside pocket.
Further on in the same discourse, he reminds
the faithful at Rome of their special privilege.   "Though the whole Church, which is
spread throughout the world ought to abound
in all virtues, yet you especially, above all
people, it behooves to excel in the works of
piety, because founded as you are upon the
very citadel of the Apostolic Rock, not only
has our Lord Jesus Christ redeemed you in
common with all men, but the blessed Apostle Peter has instructed you far beyond all
men." [2]

It is surely worth while to note here the
concept Leo had of his office, as that concept

[1] Serm. III.
[2] Ibid.

is revealed in his relations with bishops outside the Roman province. Writing to the
bishop of Aquileia in whose province the Pe-
lagian heresy had been spreading he says:
"By our authoritative injunction, we charge
you to have a care that a council of priests
of your province be convoked. . . . Let
them (those who had been too hastily received back after being guilty of heresy),
announce by full and clear statements, that
they embrace and entirely approve all the
conciliar decrees which the authority of the
Apostolic See has ratified." [1] The following extracts from his letter to Anastasius the
bishop of Thessalonica are most valuable in
this connection. "Now, therefore, dear
brother, that your request has been made
known to us through our son Nicholaus the
presbyter, that you too, like your predeces-
sors, might receive from us in our turn, jurisdiction over Illyricum for the observance of
the ordinances, *we give our consent,* and earnestly exhort, that no concealment and no
negligence may be allowed in the government
of the churches located in Illyricum *which we
commit to you in our stead,"* etc. . . . Let
any bishop, who contrary to *our command,* is
ordained by his metropolitan without your

[1] Ep. I.

cognizance, know that he has no acknowledged
rank with us, and that they who have pre-
sumed thus to act, must render an account of
their presumption." . . . If any very
important question spring up, such as cannot
be disposed of there under your leadership,
send word to us, and seek our direction, so
that we may send word back under the Lord's
direction . . . that by our decision, we may
emphasize our right of supervision, in accord
with the ancient established tradition, and
the reverence which is due the Apostolic See:
for as we wish you to to exercise your authority in our stead, so we reserve to ourselves
points which cannot be immediately settled,
as well as persons who have appealed to
us." [1] In one of his epistles to Flavian of
Constantinople, he rebukes the latter for not
sending him a detailed account of the case of
Eutyches, and finally demands the same
"Signify to us in a full account, by the hand
of the most fit and competent person, what
innovation has sprung up against the ancient
faith, which needed to be punished with such
severity (i. e., the sentence of Flavian against
Eutyches). For the administration of the
Church, and the pious faith of our most godly
prince demand, that we manifest much con-

[1] Ep. VI.

cern for the peace of Christendom: that dissensions may be dissipated and the Catholic Faith be kept uninjured, and that those whose faith has been proved may be fortified by our authority," etc.   Leo complains to the Emperor Theodosius II of the tardiness of Flavian in answering his communication, though it appears, with some injustice to Flavian, who furnished in a letter of considerable length what Leo demanded.   We find the following words in Flavian's document: "Therefore, most holy Father, use your accustomed promptness . . . and in defending the commonweal and good of the holy churches, consent by your own letter, to approve the resolution that has been canonically passed upon him. . . . The matter now only requires your authority and concurrence, which through your wisdom will bring about general peace and quietude. For thus both the heresy that has sprung up, and the disorder which it has aroused, will easily be appeased by God's assistance through an epistle from you; and the much talked of council will also be prevented, and so the most holy churches throughout the world need suffer no disturbance." [1]

I could readily add a number of such testi-

[1] Epist. XXVI, inter Leonis magni epistolas.

monies, but the above are sufficient for our purpose. Perhaps the most unmistakable view of his prerogative as bishop of Rome, is seen in his utter rejection of the twenty-eighth canon of Chalcedon, whereby the council wished to advance the prestige of New Rome. This canon, though supported by the Emperor Marcion and the Empress Pulcheria, was summarily rejected by Leo, and though it has been stated that in giving the reason for his action he confused the decrees of Nicæa with those of Sardica, this is nothing to the point. Leo withstood an ecumenical council to defend the prerogatives of Peter's Chair. To the Empress he wrote these memorable words: "The resolution of the bishops, which is against the Nicene decree, by the authority of the blessed Apostle Peter, I absolutely annul and declare invalid."[1] And writing to the Emperor Marcion he thus refers to Anatolius, who had been raised to the see of Constantinople by Leo's favor. "Let Anatolius be content that, by the aid of your piety and *my favor and approval* he has obtained the bishopric of so great a city."[2]

If there were any vain-glorious or jealous motives prompting Leo in his bold assertion of the honors and powers attaching to his see,

[1] Ep. CV.   [2] Ep. CIV.

surely history does not reveal them. From
the day of his first words as bishop of Rome,
amid the splendid ceremonial of his consecra-
tion, until his death, his various utterances
concerning the supremacy of the Roman bishopric, manifest a deep-seated consciousness,
that that supremacy rested upon no other
than a divine foundation. It is strange that
our brilliant editor omitted to explain why
the bishops of Thessalonica, Alexandria (Cy-
ril), Aquileia and even Constantinople did
not oppose resistance to the "lofty words"
of Leo, declaring that he invaded their rights
and privileges. Again, why does Dr. Coxe
single out Leo I, who was consecrated A. D.
440 as the first great offender, so to speak.
His attitude towards Leo is much severer
than that which he adopted towards Victor,
Dionysius and Stephen. We suspect the reason, however. But to confine ourselves to
post-Nicene times, it must even then be maintained, that Leo was not the first incumbent
of the Roman See who spoke "great swelling
words of vanity." Does not Dr. Coxe recol-
lect the letter of Pope Damasus to the bishops assembled at Constantinople, in which he
commends their regard for the Apostolic See
and calls them his sons? Why does our val-
iant foe ignore Pope St. Siricius (A. D. 385)

who writes, "We carry the burden of all who
are laden; or rather the blessed Apostle Peter beareth them in us, who we believe pro-
tects and defends in all things, *us who are
the heirs of his government.*" [1] Innocent I
appears fully as guilty as the great Leo.
"Diligently and agreeably" he writes to the
Council of Milevis (A. D. 417) do you seek
counsel from the arcana of Apostolical dignity, the dignity of him on whom, besides
those things which are without, falls the care
of all the churches; following the form of the
ancient rule, which you know as well as I,
has been preserved always by the whole
world." [2] St. Celestine I (A. D. 425) writing to the Illyrican bishop says, "*We* have
an especial care about all persons, on whom
in the holy Apostle Peter Christ laid the
necessity of making all men our care, when
he gave him the Keys." Is it not amazing
that history records no protest on the part
of the bishops throughout the world, or at
least in Illyria and the East, against this
monstrous presumption on the part of Rome?
No, it is not strange because those bishops
knew the divine constitution of the Church,
and were Catholics, neither of which can be

[1] Coustant Epp. Pont., p. 624.
[2] Ibid., pp. 896, 1064.

said of Dr. Coxe. Dr. Coxe has studied his case poorly indeed, but after all as well as the case deserved, for verily it was a poor case.

It will be much to our purpose to quote here a few lines from a letter written by the historian Theodoret to Leo I, witnessing his appreciation of the special honor and juris-diction attaching to the Chair of Peter. Theodoret was bishop of Cyrus and his letter begs the annulment by Leo, of certain decrees of the Latrocinium. The letter has all the more force, proceeding as it does from an oriental source. "If Paul . . . hastened to the great Peter in order that he might carry from him the solution of difficulties to those at Antioch . . . much more do we men of little account, hasten to your Apos-tolic See, in order to obtain from you a rem-edy for the wounds of the churches. For every reason is it fitting for you to hold the first place, since your see is endowed with so many special privileges. . . . In these days God has adorned the throne of the Apostles, by placing on it your holiness, emitting as you do the rays of orthodoxy." He then pro-ceeds with the narrative of his grievances, namely the imputation of heresy and the loss of his see, and ends by a fervid appeal to Leo

for help. "I await the sentence of your
Apostolic See. I beseech and implore your
holiness to help me in my appeal to your fair
and righteous tribunal. Command me to
come to you, to prove that my teaching follows the footprints of the apostles. . . .
Do not spurn my prayer, I beg of you. Before all I implore you to tell me whether I
must bear this unrighteous decision or not.
I await your decision." [1] This testimony is
too eloquent to stand in need of either note
or commentary.

"Ambition once entering the pale of Catholicity," continues Dr. Coxe, "we find a
counter idea to that of the councils at the
root of the first usurpation of unscriptural
dignity. John 'the Faster' bishop of New
Rome . . . called himself 'Ecumenical
Bishop.' Gregory was then bishop of 'Old
Rome,' and that was the time to assert the
principle of the Decretals, had any such idea
ever been heard of. How did he meet his
brother's arrogance? Not appealing to decretals; not by asserting that such was his
own dignity derived from St. Peter, but by
protesting against such abasement of all
other patriarchs, and all other bishops (who
were all equals), and by pronouncing the im-

[1] Ep. CXIII ad Leonen Ep. Romae.

pious assumption of such a nefarious title, to denote a forerunner of Antichrist. Plainly, then, there was no Pope known to Christendom at the close of the sixth century." [1] Gregory the Great both repudiated the title of "universal bishop" for himself, and forbade its use by John of Constantinople. Without at all minimizing to the smallest extent the prerogatives of the Apostolic See, he regarded the use of such a title on the part of St. Peter's successors, as unseemly—ill fitted to him who above all others in the Church of Christ should be a pattern of humility. The assumption of such a title on the part of any other bishop, Gregory regarded as an intolerable arrogance. Although we have already quoted sufficiently from the letters of St. Gregory to show with unmistakable clearness, that Gregory regarded himself as head of the Church in the matter of jurisdiction as well as that of honor, yet, since there is much valuable testimony along the same line to be drawn from St. Gregory anent the assumption on the part of John "the Faster," of the proud title in question, I deem it proper to adduce at least a portion of it here.

"With what daring or with what inflation of pride I know not," writes Gregory to John,

[1] Ante-Nicene Fathers. Vol. VIII, p. 602.

"you have attempted to assume a new title, whereby the hearts of all your brethren might have taken scandal. . . . With regard to this same matter, weighty letters were addressed to your holiness, by our predecessor, Pelagius of holy memory; in which he annulled the acts of the synod which had been assembled among you, in the case of our once brother and fellow-bishop Gregory, because of that execrable title of pride. . . . But after his death when, I, unworthy though I be *succeeded to the government of the Church* . . . I addressed your Holiness wishing you to restrain yourself from such presumption . . . that I might first appeal to your Holiness through a sense of shame, *with this end in view however, that if the detestable and profane assumption could not be corrected through shame, rigorous canonical measures should then be resorted to.*" [1] Can the reader imagine Gregory thus addressing one whom he looked upon *as his equal?* On what ground dared Pope Pelagius annul the synod held at Constantinople, —thus interfering with the prestige of New Rome? And why in heaven's name did not the orientals cry out and protest against Roman arrogance? These queries place insur-

[1] Greg. Ep. XVIII ad Joan.

mountable difficulties in the way of accept-
ing Dr. Coxe's pet theory of the "parity of
bishops." "Was it not true," continues
Gregory, "as your Fraternity knows, that the
venerable Synod of Chalcedon offered to the
prelates of this Apostolic See, which by God's
dispensation I serve, the honor of being called
'universal bishops.' Yet not one of them
has wished to be called by such a title." [1] It
is of interest to note here that the Council of
Chalcedon actually called Leo I "οἰκουμενικὸς
ἀρχιεπίσκοπος." [2]

"To all who know the gospel it is apparent,
that by our Lord's voice, the care of the
whole Church was committed to the holy
Apostle and Prince of all the Apostles, Peter.
. . . So he received the keys of the heav-
enly kingdom, and power to bind and loose is
given to him, and the care and principality
of the whole Church is committed to him, and
yet he is not called the universal apostle." [3]
In a letter to Natalis, the bishop of Salona,
Gregory complains bitterly of the former's
disregard of the mandates of the Holy See,
and adds that "if any of the four patriarchs
had acted similarly, such great contumacy
could not by any means have been suffered to

[1] Ep. XVIII Greg. ad Joan.
[2] Labbe et Cossart Concilia.   Vol. IV, Col. 368.
[3] Ep. XXI.

go by without the most grievous scandal." [1]
"Quod si quilibet ex quatuor patriarchis fe-
cisset, sine gravissimo scandalo tanta contu-
macia transire nullo modo potuisset."

It is nothing short of astounding, to read
in the face of the foregoing testimonies the
cool remark of Dr. Coxe that "it is quite plain
that there was no 'pope' known to Christendom at the close of the sixth century. No
Protestant historian has ever had the temerity to commit himself to such a preposterous
position, and it is worthy of note that an
Anglican editor of St. Gregory's works states
as a historical fact, that the same holy pontiff
both claimed and exercised universal jurisdiction in the Church." [2]

The rest of Dr. Coxe's notes we may profit-
ably ignore. They contain nothing that has
not been put forward again and again. His
bold strokes on the question of the Forged
Decretals avail nothing, for the fraud of
those documents had been exposed by Catholic investigation long before they were ever
mentioned in Protestant controversial literature. Nicholas of Cusa, the distinguished
cardinal and theologian of the fifteenth century, not only called the Pseudo-decretals into

[1] Ep. LII.
[2] Gregory's Pastoral Life and Selected Letters. J.
Barmby, D.D., Prologom. XI.

question, but in fact opened the way to all subsequent investigation of the subject. It is a fact which should arrest attention that the exposure of the Decretals, never for a moment shook the power of the Papacy, or injured its position a jot or a tittle. The Papacy needed no apologists in the ninth century when the Forged Decretals *as a collection* first saw the light. I say "as a collection" advisedly, since it is beyond all legitimate argument that some of the documents found in the collection are genuine. The worthlessness of the Decretals *could not* affect the papal power, since that power was a great central fact known and acknowledged by both East and West ages before Nicholas I saw the light. The assertion of Dr. Coxe that Nicholas created the Papacy is too utterly childish to merit any notice in a serious discussion. Methinks, after perusing the notes of our hero, that he would have been a willing worker at the "forging" business, had the forgeries attuned themselves to his prejudices. He would not have deceived the judicious however, for he was an egregious bungler.

CHAPTER VII

VOICES FROM THE EAST

It has been a favorite contention with Anglican controversialists, that the Eastern Church never allowed the "Roman pretension," and that even a certain πρέσβεία was grudgingly accorded the successor of St. Peter. It will be of both value and interest I think, to close this little book with a few striking oriental testimonies against the above contention, especially since they are drawn from a period at which Dr. Coxe blandly states "there was no 'pope' known to Christendom."

Stephen the bishop of Dora in Palestine, was commissioned by his metropolitan the patriarch of Jerusalem, St. Sophronius, to present a document in person to Pope St. Martin, at the Lateran Council A. D. 649. Speaking of the troubles brought upon the patriarchate of St. Sophronius by Monothelitism, he says. "And for this cause sometimes we asked for water to our head, and to our eyes a fountain of tears, sometimes the wings of a dove, according to holy David, that we might fly away and announce these things to the Chair which rules and presides over all, I mean to yours the head and highest for the healing of the whole wound. For this it has been accustomed to do from old, and from the beginning with its canonical or apostolical authority, because the truly great Peter, head of the Apostles, was clearly thought worthy, not only to be entrusted with the keys of heaven, alone apart from the rest, to open it worthily to believers, or to close it justly to those who disbelieve the Gospel of Grace, but because he was first commissioned to feed the sheep of the whole Catholic Church; for "Peter," saith He, "lovest thou Me? Feed my sheep." "And again, because he had in a manner peculiar and special, a faith in the Lord stronger than all and unchangeable, to be converted and to confirm his fellows and spiritual brethren when tossed about, as having been adorned by God Himself Incarnate for us with power and sacerdotal authority,' [1] Stephen declares that such too was the faith of Sophronius. He narrates that the patriarch took him up to the summit of Calvary and there solemnly

[1] Mansi X 893, quoted by Dom John Chapman, O.S.B. Dublin Review, July, 1906. The Condemnation of Pope Honorius.

charged him to make the journey to Rome.
"Swiftly pass, therefore from one end of the
world to the other, until thou come to the
Apostolic See, where are the foundations of
the holy doctrines." After repeating the
dread charge of Sophronius, Stephen de-
scribes to Pope Martin the alacrity with
which he fulfilled his mission. "Without de-
lay I made this journey for this purpose
alone; and since then thrice have I run to
your apostolic feet, urging the prayer of
Sophronius and of all, that is, that you will
assist the imperiled faith of Christians."

We possess a valuable epistle sent to Pope
Theodore I by the oriental bishops convened
in a synod at Cyprus, May 29, A. D. 643.
"To the most holy and God-confirmed Father
of Fathers, Archbishop and œcumenical
Patriarch, Lord Theodore, Sergius, least of
bishops, greeting in the Lord."

"Christ our God has instituted your apostolic chair, O holy head, as a God-fixed and
immovable foundation. For thou, as truly
spake the divine Word, art Peter, and upon
thy foundation the pillars of the Church have
been fixed, and to thee He committed the
keys of the heavens, He ordered thee to bind
and to loose with authority on earth and in
heaven. Thou art set as the destroyer of

profane heresies, as Coryphæus and leader
of the orthodox and unsullied faith. De-
spise not then, Father, the faith of our Fathers, tossed by waves and imperiled; dis-
perse the rule of the foolish with the light of
thy divine knowledge, O most holy. Destroy
the blasphemies and insolence of the new
heretics, with their novel expressions. For
nothing is wanting to your orthodox and
apostolic definition and tradition, for the
augmentation of the faith among us. For
we (O inspired one, you who hold converse
with the holy Apostles and sit with them),
believe and confess from of old since our
very swaddling clothes, teaching according
to the holy and God-bearing Pope Leo, and
declaring that 'each nature works with the
communion of the other,' " [1] etc. Again towards the conclusion of the same synodal
document we find the following: "May God,
the Creator of all, preserve for many years
our all holy Lord, for the stability of His holy
Churches, and of the orthodox faith, the good
Shepherd, who lay down your own life for
your spiritual sheep, and who chase away
the ravages of the wolf with your pastoral
staff." [2] It would be difficult to find a document addressed to the Holy See by bishops,

[1] Mansi X, 914. [2] Ibid.

since the definition of Papal Infallibility that could be compared well with this letter of an oriental synod, in the matter of setting forth a recognition of the "Petrine idea." Yet Dr. Coxe assures us that when this epistle was written there was no "pope" known to Christendom. It would be still more difficult, nay impossible, to eliminate the "Petrine idea" from the first six centuries of the Church's history and leave organic Christianity intact. Protestantism's appeal to antiquity is, as we have previously remarked in these pages, fatal to its cause. Protestantism to be logical must sweep aside the entire history of fifteen hundred years, and mutilate the New Testament beyond recognition. It must declare Christianity to have been a colossal blunder from the start. The history of Protestantism has no surprises for the observant student of history. It began by paring down and cutting off doctrines which belonged to the deposit of faith once delivered to the Saints, and it has kept on cutting and hewing until dogma has gone almost to the last vestige, for even such a truth as the divinity of Christ is freely discussed, debated and questioned. The trademark of liberal, up-to-date Christianity is the repudiation of creed.

Anglicanism is no better than any other phase of Protestantism. Save that little coterie of Ritualists who sigh for reform, and endeavor to reintroduce much of the old faith and practice, the Anglican Church is essentially Protestant, and has not the remotest affinity to Catholicism, or even to the schismatical sects of the East, and the strongest witnesses against her pretensions are the Fathers of the Church, to whom some of her sons look for support.

So like every effort against that Rock on which the Church is built Bishop Coxe's feeble efforts come to naught. It will require far more than a few uncritical and often dishonest notes, a few distortions of history and a superabundance of bitterness and animosity to destroy that most marvelous fact (no matter what the view-point) of modern history. The force of arms, the scrutiny of science, the skill of diplomacy, and the accumulated hate of nations have tried themselves against that fact. They all die, but the "fact" tremendously vital continues its mission.

"So much must the Protestant grant," says Newman, "that, if such a system of doctrine as he would now introduce ever existed in early times, it has been clean swept away as if by a deluge, suddenly, silently, and without memorial; by a deluge coming in the night, and utterly soaking, rotting, heaving up, and hurrying off every vestige of what it found in the Church." [1]

"We know the kingdom is still on earth," says the same luminous writer. "Where is it? If all that can be found of it is what can be discerned at Constantinople or Canterbury, I say, it has disappeared; and either there was a radical corruption of Christianity from the first, or Christianity came to an end in proportion as the type of the Nicene Church faded out of the world: for all we know of Christianity in ancient history, as a concrete fact, is the Church of Athanasius and his fellow bishops: it is nothing else historically but that bundle of phenomena, that combination of claims, prerogatives and corresponding acts, some of which I have recounted above. There is no help for it then; we cannot take as much as we please, and no more, of an institution which has a monadic existence. We must either give up the belief in the Church as a divine institution altogether, or we must recognize it at this day in that communion of which the Pope is head. With him alone, and round about

[1] Development of Christian Doctrine. Introduc.

him are found the claims, the prerogatives,
and duties which we identify with the kingdom set up by Christ. We must take things
as they are; to believe in a Church, is to believe in the Pope." [1]

[1] Difficulties of Anglicans, Vol. II, The Papal ch. p. 207.

INDEX

A

Abraham Echellensis 50
Achaia 32
Adriatic Sea 7
Adrumetum 61
Ægæan Sea 6
African bishops 63
Alexandria 23, 25, 37, 38, 42, 51
American " Romanism " 61
American " Romanists " 70
Anastasius, Bishop (Thessalonica) 82
Anatolius, Bishop (Constantinople) 85
Anglican Ch., etc. 54, 68, 100
Anglicanism 28, 35, 36
Anglican Reformation 28, 29, 31
Anselm St. 24
Antioch 23, 25, 88
Apostles 1, 9, 30, 31, 77, 88
Apostolic Age 37
Apostolic Canons 41
Apostolic Rock 81
Apostolic See i, 28, 43, 44, 52, 69, 82, 86
Aquileia 82, 86
Arabic Ms. of Nicene Canons 49, 50
Arius 43
Asia, churches of 33, 76
Asia Minor 7
Asclepas, Bishop (Gaza) 40

Asseman 49
" Assertio Septem Sacramentorum " 58
Athanasius St. 38, 39, 40, 51, 101
Aurelian Persecution 13
Augustine, St. (Canterbury) 24
Augustine, St. (Hippo) 4, 25, 27

B

Baluze (Benedictine Patrologist) 71, 72, 73
à Becket, St. Thomas, Bishop 24
Benedictine Edition of Fathers 72
Bernard, St. 18
Beryllus, Bishop (Bostra) 46
Beverly 55
Bohemia 57
Broad Church 36
Byzantine Capital 43, 78

C

Callistus Pope 45, 47, 53
Calvary 96
Canterbury 22, 55, 101
Carthage, See of 63
Cathedra Petri 3
Catherine of Sienna, St. 18
Celestine I, St., Pope 87
Chair of Peter 65, 88

103